CAROLINE FOX

by the same author:

Caroline Emelia Stephen, Quaker Mystic, 1834-1909
(privately published, Birmingham, 1978)

CAROLINE FOX

Quaker Blue-stocking

1819 - 1871

friend of John Stuart Mill, Thomas and Jane Carlyle and Frederick Denison Maurice and helper of sailors in distress.

Robert J. N. Tod

William Sessions Limited
York, England
1980

© R. J. N. Tod

First published in 1980
ISBN 0 900657 54 5

Phototypeset, printed and published by William Sessions Limited
The Ebor Press, York, England
in Times New Roman

Contents

Chapter		Page
	Acknowledgements	vi
	Family Trees	viii
I	Caroline Fox	1
II	Birth and Parentage	3
III	Childhood, 1819-35	8
IV	Calm Water, 1835-40	13
V	John Sterling, 1840-44	18
VI	The Lords of Humankind Pass By, 1840-44	28
VII	Desolation Masked, 1844-46	36
VIII	All must be Earnest, 1847-55	39
IX	Dim with Childish Tears, 1855-60	51
X	To Lose that Health, 1861-71	58
	Bibliography	68
	References and Notes	70
	Index	76

Acknowledgements

I HAVE RECEIVED HELP in the writing of this book from a number of people. I should like to thank in particular Ted Milligan, Librarian of the Society of Friends, London, and Professor R. L. Brett of the University of Hull Department of English and editor of the *Journal of Barclay Fox*, for their advice and encouragement.

I am very grateful to Mr. Alan Farrant, great-great-grandson of Barclay Fox, for his generosity in lending to me a manuscript book containing over 40 letters written by Caroline Fox, which threw fresh light on the later years of her life. I am also grateful to Robin Hodgkin from whom I received a copy of the first edition of the *Journals of Caroline Fox*, which contained some notes written by L. Violet Holdsworth. I wish to thank the many members of the Fox family who provided me with information about family relationships or sent me items of family news, including Miss Annette Fox, the Rev. Bernard John Gurney Fox, Commander Hubert Fox, Mrs. Belinda Beyboer, Mrs. Merthys Reiss and Mr. John Pym. Others who have given me help include Miss Wendy Monk, editor of the selection from the *Journals of Caroline Fox*, which appeared in 1972 and Mr. G. T. Knight, Cornwall County Council Local Studies Librarian.

I thank also the Library of the Society of Friends for providing the photographic print which is reproduced as the frontispiece to this book.

I should also like to acknowledge with thanks permission received from the following publishers and authors to include quotations from books:—

Messrs. Bell and Hyman and Professor R. L. Brett for quotations from *Barclay Fox's Journal,* published in 1979.

Professor R. L. Brett for several quotations from *Saved from the flames at Penjerric,* published in *The Times,* Saturday, 18th February, 1978.

Messrs. Constable & Co. for quotations from *Caroline Fox,* by Wilson Harris, published in 1944.

Commander Hubert Fox for a quotation from *Mariana's Diary*, published by the Royal Cornwall Polytechnic Society, Falmouth.

Wellesley College, Massachusetts, U.S.A. for a quotation from *John Sterling, A Representative Victorian*, by Anne Kimball Tuell, published by Collier-MacMillan in 1941.

I also acknowledge permission received from the Department of Manuscripts, The British Library for the use of the letter from Caroline Fox to Charles Kingsley.

R. T.

Family Trees

The Fox Family of Falmouth

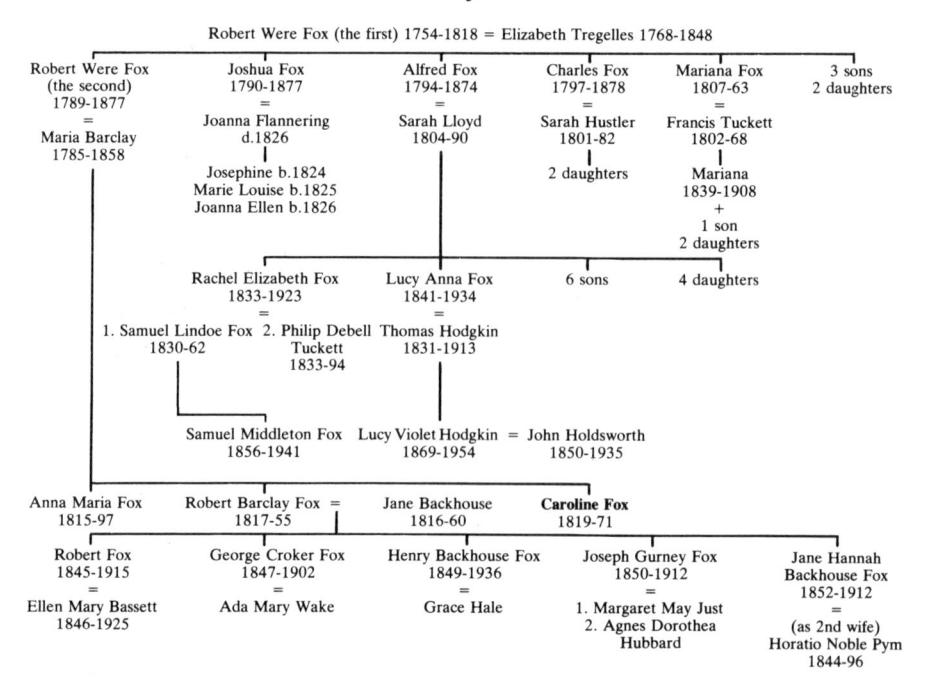

Robert Were Fox (the first) 1754-1818 = Elizabeth Tregelles 1768-1848

| Robert Were Fox (the second) 1789-1877 = Maria Barclay 1785-1858 | Joshua Fox 1790-1877 = Joanna Flannering d.1826 — Josephine b.1824, Marie Louise b.1825, Joanna Ellen b.1826 | Alfred Fox 1794-1874 = Sarah Lloyd 1804-90 | Charles Fox 1797-1878 = Sarah Hustler 1801-82 — 2 daughters | Mariana Fox 1807-63 = Francis Tuckett 1802-68 — Mariana 1839-1908 + 1 son 2 daughters | 3 sons 2 daughters |

Rachel Elizabeth Fox 1833-1923 = 1. Samuel Lindoe Fox 1830-62 2. Philip Debell Tuckett 1833-94

Lucy Anna Fox 1841-1934 = Thomas Hodgkin 1831-1913

6 sons   4 daughters

Samuel Middleton Fox 1856-1941

Lucy Violet Hodgkin 1869-1954 = John Holdsworth 1850-1935

Anna Maria Fox 1815-97

Robert Barclay Fox 1817-55 = Jane Backhouse 1816-60

Caroline Fox 1819-71

| Robert Fox 1845-1915 = Ellen Mary Bassett 1846-1925 | George Croker Fox 1847-1902 = Ada Mary Wake | Henry Backhouse Fox 1849-1936 = Grace Hale | Joseph Gurney Fox 1850-1912 = 1. Margaret May Just 2. Agnes Dorothea Hubbard | Jane Hannah Backhouse Fox 1852-1912 = (as 2nd wife) Horatio Noble Pym 1844-96 |

The Barclay Family of Bury Hill

Robert Barclay 1751-1830 = 1. Rachel Gurney 1755-94 2. Margaret Hodgson

Maria Barclay 1785-1858 = Robert Were Fox 1789-1877

| Anna Maria Fox 1815-97 | Robert Barclay Fox 1817-55 = Jane Backhouse 1816-60 | **Caroline Fox** 1819-71 |

These family trees are incomplete and have been compiled to show the names of those members of the family mentioned in the text.

CHAPTER I

Caroline Fox

FROM THE PERSPECTIVE OF TO-DAY, Caroline Fox impresses us as a literary and social phenomenon, a Quakeress who became the friend of many of the literary figures and advanced thinkers of her day, an intellectual who devoted the latter part of her life in service to her neighbours, those needing her help and sympathy.

These two facets of her personality come alive to us by two contrasting pen pictures by her near contemporaries. The first is by a cousin of a younger generation, Samuel Middleton Fox and must be based more on family tradition than on personal knowledge.

> Caroline 'burnt with a hard, gem-like flame', which was not only lit by an exceptionally brilliant mind but could, when she chose, scorch up anyone who displeased her.[1]

The second comes from the Quaker publication *The Annual Monitor*, which yearly used to record the lives of prominent Friends who had died in the preceding 12 months.

> In addition to a powerful, original and highly cultivated mind, there had been bestowed upon her gifts and graces of person and manner which helped to render her influential in a very wide and varied circle. Her deep sympathies gave her peculiar power in ministering to the poor and not to the poor only, but to the sorrowful and tried of every sort.[2]

The early years of her young adult life are well documented. There are the extracts from her journals which were edited by Horace N. Pym and published in 1882. These have provided scholars of the nineteenth century with an unexpected reservoir of information about the literary and political celebrities of her time, Wordsworth, Tennyson, Thomas and Jane Carlyle, John Stuart Mill, Elizabeth Fry and John Bright. A life, based on these Journals, by Wilson Harris was published in 1944 and a

1

selection from the *Journal* by Wendy Monk came out in 1972. Then there is the recently published edition of the *Journal* of her brother Robert Barclay Fox edited by Professor R. L. Brett, which gives her brother's view of some of the incidents described by Caroline, as well as a small amount of additional information about Caroline herself.[3]

Caroline was however a reticent person in so far as her own views and feelings were concerned. In her *Journal* there is such copious information about other people that it is hard to track down those passages which reveal her own private thoughts and her own way of life. The biography by Wilson Harris gives so much attention to the famous contemporaries whom Caroline met that her own personality remains obscured. So my task has been to reverse the emphasis of Wilson Harris in order to throw light upon the author herself rather than upon the people about whom she wrote. This has meant selection and abbreviation.

But as my acquaintance with Caroline grew, the person that emerged proved to be of different character from that usually presented. The traditional view is of a Quaker bluestocking of charm and vivacity who recorded the words of many of the literary personalities of her day. I believe that picture to be correct of only the early years of her adult life. The new picture that I have to present is of someone who had an emotional crisis in her mid twenties which altered the whole course of her subsequent years. Horace Pym in his memoir tried to conceal the crisis and Wilson Harris claimed that it caused no outward scar. A study of certain clues in the *Journal*, hitherto overlooked, and an examination of some manuscript letters dating from the later years of her life convince me that the crisis was more overwhelming than previously recognized and that it led to a new orientation in her life. So, of the two quotations given at the beginning of this chapter the first may well have been true for her young years, the second true for her later years.

CHAPTER II

Birth and Parentage

CAROLINE, THE THIRD OF A FAMILY of three children, was born in the family home, Rosehill, Falmouth, Cornwall, on the 24th May, 1819, the same day as was born another girl baby, Victoria, the Queen, who gave her name to an age.

Her parents were unusual people, belonging to an exceptional circle of cultured, devout and substantial Quakers, many of them related to each other, and all living in a cluster of family dwellings both in Falmouth and in the countryside around. Her father and mother each came from long lines of Quaker forbears and were themselves both devoted and unswerving members of the Society of Friends throughout their lives.

In other parts of England, under the influence of such Quaker leaders as the powerful Joseph John Gurney, Quakerism was coming under the sway of the evangelical trends of the time. The group of Friends in Falmouth, however, living as they did over 250 miles from London, seem to have preserved an earlier tradition of plainness, quietism and devotion to principle as well as an openness to scientific ideas and cultural influences coming from outside the Society of Friends. For them Quakerism provided a pattern of life, an emotional strength, and a secure base from which its educated members could launch out into exploration both of the expanding physical world and of the rich and diverse imaginative and literary world.

Caroline's father, Robert Were Fox, was a partner with his brothers and a cousin in a firm of shipping agents in Falmouth, which provided them with a comfortable means of living. He also had an interest in the Cornish mining industry and in mining engineering and again with his brothers started an iron foundry at Perran nearby to make machinery for the mines. Further than this he was an amateur scientist of repute and conducted scientific experiments on his living-room table. A cousin of Caroline's mother who visited the family in the 1820's has left this account:

3

> Imagine the back drawing-room strewed with reflectors, and magnets, and specimens of iron, and borax, cobalt, copper ore, blowpipes, platina, etc., etc.; deflagrations, fusions, and detonations, on every side; whilst we were deeply interested in watching the fusions of the ores, or their assaying; only that now and then I, having a house of my own, had a fellow-feeling with Maria, at seeing a certain beautiful zebra-wood table splashed with melted lead or silver, and the chased Bury Hill candlestick deluged with acids.[4]

Robert Were Fox proved by experiment extending over 40 years that the temperature in mines increased the further one descended, an increase in a constantly diminishing ratio with the increase in depth. He was also the inventor of the Deflector Dipping Needle, which made possible an improvement in the design of ships' compasses. This new compass was of great service to the ships that took part in polar exploration and was used in the voyage to the Antarctic of Ross in 1837.

Robert Fox became a member of the British Association for the Advancement of Science shortly after its foundation in York in 1831, attended their meetings whenever they were held within reach, and contributed papers on several occasions. He wrote over 60 papers for scientific journals on such subjects as the temperature in mines and on the qualities of alloys of platinum. In 1848 he was elected a Fellow of the Royal Society.

His scientific bent of mind was accompanied by an acceptance of a revealed religion, believing that the more deeply the works of God were understood, the more would difficulties and contradictions pass away. He served as an elder of the Society of Friends and the following description gives an impression of him and also of his widowed mother as they appeared in Falmouth Meeting in the year 1848.

> At the head of the meeting sat two Friends, a mother and a son, the former a minister, the latter an elder – Elizabeth Fox and her son Robert Were Fox. The mother was rather a fragile-looking old lady verging upon 80, dressed, of course in the orthodox Quaker costume – cylindrical bonnet and . . . white silk shawl, but all of the best material, and scrupulously neat. The son was already elderly, near the end of his sixth decade. His noble forehead was almost bald, but with his strongly-marked black eyebrows and beautifully carved profile, he was still and always to uttermost old age a strikingly handsome man.[5]

There is also a description of him by a niece at a still later age which conveys the qualities he had as a grandfather and must have had as a father.

> His smile was an illumination, and his quick ardour of nature as inspiring as Anna Maria's, but he was not as sanguine in his nature as she is, and in matters of thought he cautiously felt his way.... He gave one a sense of intensity and strength, and yet of a childlike simplicity, which was inexpressibly delightful, His love for children and sympathy with them made him one with the smallest playfellows.... He responded to all their different minds and natures with the brightest, tenderest warmth of fellowship. If a tiny finger ached, it was an instant cure to nestle in his arms.... His smile of welcome was something to warm one through life, and the dear open arms and eager quick step along the terrace can never grow faint in one's memory.... His mental attitude seemed as vigorous as ever at 80, and his interest as keen in everything brought before him.
>
> ... Till great illness prostrated him in the last two years of his life, he never seemed more in his element than in analysing some new discovery in science, ... or when helping the most ignorant to understand some law of nature. His patience and happy sympathy with a child's inquiries and interest about a magnet or prism, and the way in which he opened to one almost unawares the secrets of nature and science, are all vividly before me.... He never seemed to *teach*, it was as if he led one rejoicingly into the region where he was always naturally at home, and welcomed one to share in its treasures. [6]

We have two contrasting pictures of Caroline's grandmother, Elizabeth Fox, born Elizabeth Tregelles, already mentioned as a Quaker minister in Falmouth meeting. A great grandson, Samuel Fox described the character that had been handed down by family tradition:

> I fancy our great-grandmother Elizabeth Fox must have been awe-inspiring. She was a woman of masculine capacity, and it is said her young sons invited (or at least acquiesced in) her help in carrying on the business after their father's death. The result was not wholly satisfactory, and I have heard that her mining speculations were unfortunate.... Like most people of strong will and rigid principles, she was a great disciplinarian. No lenient elasticity of the Friendly conscience could be permitted. Yet she could pardon when the maternal heart was appealed to. [7]

Caroline Fox herself gives a warmer and softer picture of her grandmother in old age.

> A serene, courteous, wise and loving woman – a sort of ideal old lady and humble Christian blended into one; a woman of the most lively sympathies, the centre of a warmly attached and curiously dependent circle, mature in wisdom, childlike in love, fresh and beaming in the bright things 'scattered at our feet like flowers'. There she sat in her great arm-chair, looking perfectly serene and smiling, dressed with the utmost nicety, looking, as some one said, as if she had just stepped out of a band-box, receiving visitors of all descriptions... but I need not carve a frame for my little domestic picture, it is enough to say that many, if not all, who came near her felt it a blessing, and that she was recognized as a rallying point for all that was good amongst us.[8]

Caroline's parents were married in 1814. Her mother, three years older than her father, was Maria Barclay of Bury Hill, near Dorking, Surrey. Maria Barclay also came from Quaker forebears, being descended on her father's side from the Robert Barclay, who wrote an early text-book of the principles of Quakerism, *An Apology for the True Christian Divinity as the same is held forth and preached by the people in scorn called Quakers,* originally published in latin in 1676. Her mother was the daughter of John Gurney of Norwich and her first cousin was Elizabeth Gurney who became famous as Elizabeth Fry, the prison reformer.

Caroline never knew her maternal grandmother, Rachel Gurney who became Rachel Barclay, as this grandmother died when Caroline's own mother was still a girl. After her death, Caroline's grandfather, Robert Barclay seems to have relaxed the strictness of the Quaker upbringing his children had been given. The motherless children took part in dancing, attended concerts and did not wear the plain dress of other Quakers. After hearing ministry in Meeting for Worship, Maria began to feel that such pursuits were frivolous and inconsistent with Friends' principles. She began to read William Law's *Serious Call to a Devout Life* and found support for her views from a cousin, Priscilla Gurney, whom she visited in Norfolk. Later after meeting her cousin Elizabeth Fry and her uncle Joseph Gurney, both of them Friends who followed traditional Quaker customs of plainness of speech and dress, she experienced the change of heart that led her to decide to demonstrate to the world around her that henceforward she was a committed Quaker. This involved her in always wearing the plain unadorned Quaker grey dress and bonnet and shawl and addressing all she met by the now archaic second person singular, 'thee' and 'thou'.

After her marriage, Maria Fox was recorded by Cornwall Monthly Meeting as a Quaker minister. Maria did not share the scientific tastes of her husband, but she appears to have been a calm and serene and devoted wife and mother. A niece wrote of her:

> My remembrance of my aunt in my child days is of one who drew me to her with the gentlest tenderness, and who made me hate having a naughty thought or feeling hidden anywhere when I came near her, because it seemed profane.... Her presence had a calming power, and she seemed to harmonise the most discordant elements if she came in their midst.[9]

The niece also wrote of her aunt and uncle as follows:

> I suppose, [says the same niece,] that her even sweetness and calm specially ministered to a need in him of that perfect sort of soothing balm. His vigorous strength and radiant energy rested in her reposefulness, whilst her delightful cheerfulness and bright response of mind always met his interests with lively sympathy, though his special line of objects was in many cases quite out of her own region of attention. She admired and wondered, and shared the excitement of his scientific researches and their results. The unity of their Quaker faith and practice was entire.[10]

CHAPTER III

Childhood 1819-35

SUCH WAS CAROLINE'S PARENTAGE and family. At birth, she came into a home containing a sister, Anna Maria, three years older than herself and a brother, Robert Barclay, two years older. The small amount of information that we have about her as a young child comes from a cousin of her mother's, Mary Anne Schimmel-Penninck, born a Quaker and married to a Dutch merchant. She left this description in a letter quoted by Horace Pym: 'Caroline is quick, bright and susceptible, with little black laughing eyes, a merry round face, and as full of tricks and pranks as a marmozet, or Shakespeare's Robin Goodfellow'.[11] In old age her sister, Anna Maria, used to carry a marmozet to her Quaker meeting, hidden in her muff. Her brother, Barclay, when a boy, had some pet monkeys, which could have been marmozets, so the comparison was no doubt based on observation.

Mary Anne Schimmel-Penninck visited the Fox family in 1824 when Caroline would have been five years old and gave this picture of the children's morning expedition to the beach.

> Then I used to hear the trampling of many little feet, as the three children, and their maid, and Frances and Emma, with Maria Fox, and a mule to assist in carrying the weary ones, used to set out in company, down the garden, and through the lane, to the beach, where, alone in the midst of the rocks and the caverns, and with no spectators but the shags and the sea-gulls, they used to bathe.
>
> It was pleasant to me, as I was dressing, to watch them coming back, winding along the cliffs; and, as they drew near, Maria, seated on her mule, with little Carry in her arms, Anna Maria by her side, and the others surrounding her, repeating their hymns and psalms, they used to look just like Raffaelle's picture of the Holy Family in the flight to Egypt. Maria's holy and maternal countenance on these occasions I shall never forget; nor the sweet and tender emotion of her children. Little Carry, especially, used

to enjoy the ride. 'O Mamma,' said she, one day, 'do let me say my hymn louder, for the poor mule is listening, and cannot hear me.' Their return I used soon to know by Carry or Barclay besetting me, the moment I opened my door, to tell them stories of wild beasts.

At half-past eight the loud stroke of a Chinese gong called the whole household to assemble for reading.[12]

Information about the next few years of her childhood is sparse, but the unexpected discovery, in 1977, of the volume of a journal, which Caroline began to write in January 1832, gives us some new light on this period of her life. Her father invited each of the children to keep a journal and promised them the reward of a sovereign if they kept them up to the end of the year. Caroline continued faithfully to write a journal till near the end of her life; naturally it filled several volumes. It was believed that these original manuscript volumes had been consumed by the flames when in 1897 the family made a bonfire of all the red-bound books of her *Journal* they could find. This one volume, bound in marble covers, escaped, but had remained undetected until it was discovered at Penjerrick, the country home of the Fox family. Further light is given in the *Journal* of her brother Barclay Fox, recently published.

From these two sources we learn about Caroline's education. Living in a cultured home with a scientist father, the three children must have received plenty of intellectual stimulation. In 1832, in the same year as the opening of her *Journal*, Caroline joined her brother and sister in a schoolroom at Rosehill. A tutor, John Richards, was engaged and there was a visiting French tutor, Alfeston, and a drawing master, Thomas Jordan. Another pupil from Falmouth, Cavendish Wall, also attended the lessons. Caroline, aged 12, and Anna Maria, aged 15, seemed to have covered some of the same subjects as the boys. These included mathematics, history, geography, scripture, poetry and French. Caroline and Anna Maria also went to a lady in Falmouth for private tuition in Italian and at some time Caroline must also have learned German. In her father's house science was of course not neglected and Robert Were Fox taught the children himself: astronomy, geology and chemistry. Caroline must have been a lively child to teach and we learn from Barclay's *Journal* that she was not always a model pupil. He records, 'Carry was turned out of the schoolroom to-day for laughing'.[13]

Then there was the writing of 'themes'. Every week the children were given a theme to write; these themes were read aloud on Saturdays and each child was given a mark. Sometimes the parents took a part in the writing of the themes and read them out with the children. Themes mentioned included Humility, Forgiveness, Tolerance, Curiosity, Preserving Health; but also more concrete subjects were chosen such as an account of glass-making which they had seen on a visit to Bristol.

Normally the writing of themes would involve the children in consulting books in the family library or elsewhere and working out their own ideas. Sometimes there were short cuts. On one occasion Caroline confided to her *Journal,* 'Papa said my theme on humility was the best I had ever written. Extra Private, half of it was copied from the Encyclopedia & the other half from the Bible'.[14] Sometimes they were required to write their themes in verse but the children found this a burden and in response to their protests this custom was abandoned. Caroline and Anna Maria also did needlework with their mother and accompanied her on her visits to 'poor people'. One day's routine is described as follows:

> Got up at 6 o'clock A.M. & [I] went down to the coach with our 3 beloved cousins [the Gurney children from Ham House, Upton]. We grieved to part & longed again to meet–but as grieving was useless we cheered up & fortunately no time was given us for sorrow for from 9 to 10 we were with Richards 10 to 11 with Alfeston 11 to 12 reading & working with Mamma. 12 to 2 with Jordan 2 to 4 paying calls & talking. (Middy [probably one of the maids] was married at the Bank [Bank House, the home of her grandmother] today & we went to congratulate her) 4 to $\frac{1}{2}$ past at dinner, $\frac{1}{2}$ + 4 to $\frac{1}{2}$ + 5 writing theme & $\frac{1}{2}$ + 5 to 9 busy walking & talking with the Wodehouses who took tea here. So ends a busy day.[15]

For exercise Caroline and Anna Maria played cricket with the boys, practised archery, and enjoyed bathing. Caroline had some of the usual childish ailments, toothache and whooping cough. The latter illness was treated with three leeches on her side. These apart, her health seems to have been normal.

Then every other year the family went to London for the Friends Yearly Meeting. She describes the journey to London in 1834 as follows:

> Went away at 8 o'clock. Aunt L[ucy] was in very good spirits. We set off in the carriage and gig and Granny's horses and had a charming ride to Truro where we all settled in the carriage [the horses and gig would then have returned to Falmouth] and passed through Bodmin, Lanceston, Oakhampton and got to tea at Exeter at 11 o'clock, where we were glad to get to bed . . . we went 96 miles.

The next entry reads:

> Got up after a good night's rest and breakfasted at Honiton. Passed through Bridport just before which we went through a very curious tunnel at Charmouth, bought some curious specimens. Read some of Mrs Somerville and thought it 'mighty improving'–Got to Salisbury at a quarter after 10 to tea after passing many new roads and enjoying a nice dinner in the carriage. I rode one stage outside with Kitty [the lady's maid] which was truly charming. We were glad to get to Salisbury after travelling 90 miles. One of the first acts was one truly praiseworthy, viz. blowing out the wax candles and ordering mould ones, no fuss.[16]

The home in which Caroline grew up was a surprisingly cultured and literary one for a Quaker family of the time. Samuel Middleton Fox gives us this vivid picture:

> When as a small boy paying a timid visit, I saw a copy of Guido's *Aurora* hanging in the drawing-room, bound copies of the *Athenæum* on the shelves, and knick-knacks from Rome on the table; when I heard the second part of Goethe's *Faust* discussed at the luncheon-table under a print of Raphael's 'Sposalizio della Madonna', a new world of wonder opened before me.[17]

The family were however surrounded by other members of the Fox family with similar interests and styles of living.

Chief among them were Caroline's two uncles Alfred and Charles Fox, both of them partners in the shipping firm. Alfred had married Sarah Lloyd daughter of Samuel Lloyd of Lloyd's Bank of Birmingham and they had a family of 12 children. Charles had married Sarah Hustler from the north of England and they had two daughters of whom one died in childhood. Aunt Charles had spent her childhood in the Lake District and knew the Wordsworths and the Coleridges.

Alfred, like Caroline's father, was a scientist and a mineralogist and also a mathematician. He was known for his clear head and business ability and for his perfect temper and sweet disposition. He had a house at Wodehouse Place, Falmouth, and a country 'cottage' a few miles out at Glendurgan.

Charles had a literary bent, owned a large library, was a judge of paintings and kept up to date with scientific discoveries. He was one of the founders of the Royal Cornwall Polytechnic Society. He served as an elder of the Society of Friends and travelled on the continent of Europe as a companion to Quaker ministers. He also visited Palestine to see the sites associated with the life of Jesus.

As far as Caroline is concerned it was her Uncle Charles and also Aunt Charles who feature most in her *Journal*. They were frequently in London with the Robert Foxes at the time of Yearly Meeting and accompanied the young people on some of their visits to the Carlyles. It was Aunt Charles who secured for them an introduction to the poet Wordsworth.

The odd man out in this circle was Uncle Joshua. He had married a French girl, Joanna Flannering, and had been disowned by the Society of Friends. His three daughters, two of them with French names, seemed to be a little withdrawn from the Quaker world. Uncle Joshua lost his wife a short time after his marriage and lived almost the life of a hermit in a country retreat at Tregedna, surrounded by flowers and birds. Caroline wrote about him as follows:

> We were delighted to watch Uncle Joshua in his sweet companionship with Nature; the little birds are now so intimate and trustful that they come when he calls them and eat crumbs out of his mouth. It is a charming and beautiful sight.[18]

CHAPTER IV

Calm Water, 1835-40

WRITING IN HER *Journal* on 1st January, 1840, Caroline said 'we have been hitherto in calm water indeed, and for this how thankful should we be, but we must expect some gales before we drop our anchor'.[19] Caroline's premonitions were fulfilled a few years later, but her years from the age of 15 to 21 seem to have been spent in calm water.

In 1871 after her death, the family invited Horace N. Pym, a solicitor, related to the family by his two marriages, to make a selection from Caroline's journals for publication. Horace Pym selected those entries in which Caroline described her encounters with the notable people who would be of interest to the reading public of the time, scientist friends of her father, writers, some politicians, conversationalists or curious characters. This selection was published in 1882 on fine paper in a handsome quarto volume with the title of *Memories of Old Friends, being extracts from the journals and letters of Caroline Fox of Penjerrick, Cornwall, from 1835 to 1871,* although on the spine of the book appears the simpler title *Caroline Fox her Journals and Letters.*

Until this book appeard, Caroline Fox must have been quite unknown beyond a small circle, so judging that it was Caroline's views on others rather than of herself which would interest the public, Horace Pym selected but few entries which throw light upon her own thoughts and feelings. He was also no doubt guided by a suitable sense of reticence in revealing the private life of someone who had died so recently and whose father and elder sister were still alive. Consequently the most significant occurrence in Caroline's life, her relationship with John Sterling, ending with her withdrawal from an engagement of marriage and then his subsequent death, is nowhere directly mentioned.

Caroline however did give her readers some private revelations of her feelings which Horace Pym reproduced in his volume, probably without understanding their significance. These are the few lines from a poem or prose quotation which Caroline selected and copied out as the first entry for every new year, to serve, as she says, as her motto or watchword for the year. These inevitably tell us of the thoughts that absorbed her as she entered a new year and so throw light upon the occurrences of the year that had passed. Previous writers on Caroline Fox do not appear to have grasped their significance. Examples of such mottoes will be given as they occur to illustrate her prevailing attitudes.

Her life from the age of 16 to 21 was spent largely in the family home, Rosehill, Falmouth. The house still stands to-day, a substantial but unpretentious Georgian house with its solidity relieved by a graceful semi-circular porch supported upon slender columns. The house looks down over a rich unfolding garden of rare trees and shrubs, now diminished in size. We have a description of the house and garden by a French visitor who came to stay some years later. Speaking of Caroline's father he says:

> His home contains magnificent pictures, rare china and a rich collection of animals; but I was more struck by the beauty of his gardens, which have justly been compared with those of the Hesperides. The orange, date and lemon trees pass the winter here in the open air, grow freely and bare ripe fruit. I saw a tree there from which 123 lemons were plucked in one day, all excellent, and much sweeter than those sold at the shops. Mr. Fox has naturalized more than 300 exotic species; he has thus brought together the plants of Australia and New Zealand, the trees of cold countries and those of hot countries, loaded all the year round with flowers and fruit; large aloes, not imprisoned in a box or under glass houses, but planted freely in the ground . . . they grow as if they were at home.[20]

The family also owned a farm at Penjerrick, near Falmouth. This became the responsibility of Barclay when he reached the age of 20 and father and son worked together, planning a garden there and planting fine trees. Later the house and garden became the family's usual residence during the summer months.

At Rosehill or at Penjerrick her parents received visitors to Falmouth, some of them scientific friends of her father, perhaps fellow members of the British Association, or at times visitors travelling to or from the port of Falmouth. We may imagine Caroline as a quiet listener to all the talk that went on, memorizing words and phrases and observing mannerisms and appearances and then later in her bedroom catching these occasions in apt and descriptive words in her *Journal*. At times she can pin-point a character and at times uncover attitudes that lie below the surface. For instance of Henry de la Beche, a visiting geologist who became a near neighbour she says, 'De la Beche came in at breakfast-time and was a regular fun-engine'.[21] Then some days later she comments on 'the artificial spirits in which he so often seems to be veiling his griefs and disappointments'.[22] In writing of John Moultrie, a now forgotten nineteenth-century poet she says, 'He talks as if it were too much trouble to arrange his words, but out they tumble, and you gladly pick them up and pocket them for better or for worse'.[23]

The *Journal* entries selected for publication rarely mention her own views or contributions and probably at this period of her life the motto for 1839 from Milton, epitomises her attitude.

> I was all ear,
> And took in strains that might create a soul
> Under the ribs of death.[24]

It so happens that a few days before recording this motto she does mention for the first time her taking part in an argument. It was on the merits of Radicals and of Radicalism and she says 'We argued a little. . . .'[25]

She also made contact with visitors through her autograph book. We may imagine her coming forward before her father's guests departed to show them her book and to invite them to sign their names or to present an autographed letter from a well-known person.

The motto from James Thomson's *The Seasons* that she chose for the year 1835, when she was not yet 16, probably gives the flavour of how she felt during these years.

> Home is the resort
> Of love, of joy, of peace and plenty, where,
> Supporting and supported, polish'd friends
> And dear relations mingle into bliss'[26]

All her days at this time were not filled with encounters with notable people and recording her observations upon them. When Caroline was but 16, she and Anna Maria started a small paper called *The Falmouth Foolscap* 'containing Politics, Advertisements, Puffs & Varieties extraordinary with all the other component parts of a popular paper & the valuable addition of illustrations'.[27] It is not clear whether the paper was just for family circulation or whether it was actually printed.

Caroline and Anna Maria and Barclay enjoyed walking and explored the cliffs of the sea coast in search of geological specimens; they also studied the fortifications of the nearby castles. When 16 she mentions 'a merry country excursion, the geological part of which was extremely satisfactory to all parties'.[28] Her motto by Thomas May for 1837 expresses her love of the countryside.

> Then let me, fameless, love the fields and woods,
> The fruitful watered vales, and running floods.[29]

By the age of 17, Caroline had already begun to make her own visits to old people in the district. Her *Journal* for 2nd February, 1837, reads: 'Called on some of the old women. One of them said, "It was quite a frolic my coming to read to them". What different views some people have of frolics'.[30]

Caroline must then have begun to develop the sensitivity and skills in ministering to the poor and to the sorrowful and tried. During the years that were shortly to come, when Caroline was involved in literary and intellectual interests, there can have been but little time available for her social concerns, and her printed *Journal* makes scarce references to them. The recently published *Journal* of her brother however shows that her stream of compassion continued to flow even if concealed. Although the following extract belongs to the year 1841, yet it illustrates so vividly Caroline's concern and loving care that it is better included here to carry on the theme.

> 28. Sunday. This morning looking out of my window, which commands that of the servants' hall, I saw a picture which would have equally suited Wordsworth or Wilkie, Caroline teaching a poor girl to read, who was poor indeed, being blind & deaf & almost dumb. The window formed the frame of the picture & the light fell on their faces, showing the strong contrast of earnest intelligence in the one and the puzzled vacant expression of the other, which artists & poets so delight in. They were poring over a tablet, on which C. had worked in large stitches the Lord's Prayer and was guiding her hand over the letters & words which the other spelt & pronounced in her half-articulate way, now getting thoroughly aground & turning up her sightless eyes with a distressed look, & then returning to her task & now highly pleased, when C.'s approving pat on the hand told her she was right. I thought that if the poor girl learnt nothing else, yet if she learnt that one fellow being in the world took a warm interest in her welfare, forlorn & isolated & unattractive as she seemed, that alone was worth the trouble, & was enough to keep from utterly drying up those invaluable fountains of love & sympathy & gratitude without which the heart is a barren & unblessed thing.[31]

In September, 1837, the family had a holiday in Grasmere, where they had an introduction to Hartley Coleridge, the son of the poet. Caroline described their first meeting with him; '. . . a little being was observed at the door, standing hat in hand, bowing to the earth round and round, and round again, with eyes intensely twinkling – it was Hartley Coleridge'.[32] He offered to act as their cicerone and took them to Rydal Mount to visit William Wordsworth, but they found only Mary Wordsworth at home who took them over their exquisite grounds. In Hartley Coleridge's company they 'idly talked and idly listened, and drank in meanwhile a sense of the perfect beauty and loveliness of the nature around us'.[33]

There were also visits to the meetings of the British Association, when it met in Bristol in 1836, when Caroline was 17, and the following year in Liverpool, when she attended a meeting of the Physical Section and heard part of a discussion on spectrum light. On both occasions her father contributed papers.

Every other year there were the journeys to London in order to attend the Yearly Meeting of the Society of Friends which met in the latter part of May and lasted about 10 days. But a visit to London also gave the young people opportunities to make a round of intellectual and social visits. In 1838 when Caroline was just 19, she attended an Anti-Slavery meeting at Exeter Hall, visited the rooms of the Royal Society at Somerset House to see scientific instruments, went to King's College to meet Professor Wheatstone and see him demonstrate his newly invented electric telegraph and finally gathered with others at the Athenaeum in order to see the coronation procession of the young queen, her age contemporary.

CHAPTER V

John Sterling, 1840-44

CAROLINE'S *Journal* FOR 8TH FEBRUARY, 1840, has this entry: 'Barclay has been much pleased with a Mr. Sterling, a very literary man, now at Falmouth, who was an intimate friend of S. T. Coleridge during the latter part of his life'.[34]

From that date for a period of four years John Sterling and Caroline Fox were frequently in each other's company and there is no doubt that he became the most important intellectual stimulus in her life, expanding her knowledge of books and authors, of philosophy and politics and forming her literary and artistic taste. A friendship starting as an intellectual companionship must have gradually progressed into a tender relationship, leading eventually, after the death of Sterling's wife, to a proposal of marriage and possibly to an understanding or even engagement for a short time.

In February 1840, Caroline was not yet 21 and John Sterling was 33 and had been married for nine years, seemed a devoted husband and already had five children. John Sterling had come to Falmouth on his way to Madeira, intending to spend the rest of the winter in a mild climate to benefit his health. Stormy weather prevented his sailing on the Madeira packet and so Sterling stayed on in Falmouth for the next two or three months, his wife and family remaining at Clifton, near Bristol.

If John Sterling is at all remembered to-day, it is as the subject of an out-spoken, blustering, and very readable biography by Thomas Carlyle. But this was the second biography of Sterling to be published. The first was by Julius Hare, Archdeacon of Lewes, at one time Sterling's tutor at Cambridge and subsequently the rector under whom Sterling served as curate. In 1848, four years after Sterling's death, Hare published a memoir of the author's life prefixed to an edition of his *Essays and Tales*. The memoir dwells largely upon Sterling's religious and philosophical views, and in places the tone is critical and moralizing. Julius Hare regretted Sterling's welcome to critical views of the Bible coming from German thinkers and in particular his partisanship for the radical picture of Jesus as a Jewish Socrates put forward in Strauss's *Life of Jesus*. To Hare, Strauss's book was anathema, 'a book which a person can hardly read without being more or less hurt by it'. And he goes on, 'If we walk through mire, some if it will stick to us . . .'[35] and he then devotes three pages to moralizing about Sterling's errors. Hare's memoir so incensed Carlyle, that he immediately set to and wrote another biography to put right the picture and this was published just three years later.

The portrait presented by Carlyle, though perhaps biased in another direction, is a clearer and more attractive one than that conveyed by Hare. John Sterling was born in 1806, the son of Edward Sterling, who later became well-known as a leader-writer in *The Times* newspaper. He was educated at Trinity College and Trinity Hall, Cambridge, where he made a brilliant mark. Then together with Frederick Denison Maurice, he bought the journal *The Athenaeum*, which they edited for a short time.

Carlyle divides Sterling's life into three major epochs. There was first a radical epoch. At Cambridge at the Union, Sterling had attacked the conservatism of the Church of England, calling for an end to superstition. The climax of this phase, 'the grand consummation and explosion of Radicalism in his life',[36] as Carlyle says, was his espousal of the cause of the Spanish refugee, General Torrijos, an upholder of democracy against oppression in Spain. Sterling succeeded in finding arms and a boat for Torrijos and sending him to Gibraltar and thence to Spain, where General Torrijos and all his companions were summarily executed. Sterling himself had been all set to accompany Torrijos, but was held back by ill-health and by his marriage in 1830 to Susannah Barton. It was a tragic incident in Sterling's life, of which he rarely spoke in later years.

During this time, Sterling had become the disciple of Samuel Taylor Coleridge, poet and by this time established in Highgate as a sort of prophet, where visitors came to listen to what Carlyle calls his 'moonshine'. Through listening to Coleridge, Sterling convinced himself that he could reconcile his critical and radical views on politics and church affairs with acceptance of the traditions of the Church of England. This was the second epoch of this life. He took deacon's orders and became curate to Julius Hare at Herstmonceux, Sussex. He stayed there but eight months and then resigned his post, partly for reasons of health, but according to Carlyle because he found that such a calling was an aberration in his life.[37] He then entered upon the third epoch, devotion to literature.

From childhood, John Sterling had suffered from a pulmonary disease, no doubt tuberculosis. This afflicted him throughout his life and restricted his activities severely. He found his condition alleviated by spending the winter months of each year in warmer climates and so there came about what Carlyle called his peregrinities. These were his residence with his family for 15 months in 1831 in the island of St. Vincent, and the winters of 1836 to 1838 spent in Bordeaux, Madeira and Italy.

John Sterling was the author of a novel, *Arthur Coningsby*, a tragedy *Strafford* and a number of essays, stories and poems. He was an admirer and friend of Carlyle, but for his part Carlyle thought little of his poems, saying that his 'verses had a monotonous rub-a-dub, instead of tune'.[38] To-day his prose works are also forgotten.

The gift which impressed his contemporaries most was his talk and we have many witnesses to his brilliance both in formal debate and in general conversation. Barclay Fox wrote in his *Journal* in 1841.

> His eloquence was like a clear cascade. His knowledge seems almost universal. You name a writer or an event and he can tell you all the details. His mind is European, his liberality unbounded. His insight of character is like an infallible instinct, his imagination rich to overflowing. To know him is a privilege the highest might be proud of; to know what he knows were an affluence few could safely bear.[39]

Thomas Carlyle describes his conversation as follows:

> A beautiful childlike soul! He was naturally a favourite in conversation, especially with all who had any funds for conversing: frank and direct, yet polite and delicate withal,—though at times too he could crackle with his dexterous petulancies, making the air all like needles round you; and there was no end to his logic when you excited it; no end, unless in some form of silence on your part. Elderly men of reputation I have sometimes known offended by him: for he took a frank way in the matter of talk; spoke freely out of him, freely listening to what others spoke, with a kind of 'hail fellow well met' feeling; and carelessly measured a man much less by his reputed account in the bank of wit, or in any other bank, than by what the man had to show for himself in the shape of real spiritual cash on the occasion. But withal there was ever a fine element of natural courtesy in Sterling; his deliberate demeanour to acknowledged superiors was fine and graceful; his apologies and the like, when in a fit of repentance he felt commanded to apologize, were full of naivety, and very pretty and ingenuous.[40]

In May of the same year 1841, Caroline, as she says, tried her hand at writing a description of his appearance as well as his conversation:

John Sterling is a man of stature, not robust, but well-proportioned; hair brown and clinging closely round his head; complexion very pale, eyes grey, nose beautifully chiselled, mouth very expressive. His face is one expressing remarkable strength, energy, and refinement of character. In argument he commonly listens to his antagonist's sentiments with a smile, less of conscious superiority than of affectionate contempt (if such a combination may be)—I mean what would express, 'Poor dear! she knows no better!' In argument on deep or serious subjects, however, he looks earnest enough, and throws his ponderous strength into reasoning and feeling: small chance then for the antagonist who ventures to come to blows! He can make him and his arguments look so small; for, truth to tell, he dearly loves this indomitable strength of his; and I doubt any human power bringing him to an acknowledgment of mistake with the consequent conviction that the opposite party was right. Sterling possesses a quickness and delicacy of perception quite feminine, and with it a power of originating deep and striking thoughts, and making them the foundation of a regular and compact series of consequences and deductions such as only a man, and a man of extraordinary power of close thinking and clearness of vision, can attain unto. He is singularly uninfluenced by the opinions of others, preferring, on the whole, to run counter to them than make any approach to a compromise.[41]

This was the John Sterling, who was to fill the horizon of Caroline's life for the next four years. He came into the circle of the Fox family as the friend of Barclay and became the close companion of the three young people, Anna Maria, 24, Barclay, 23, and Caroline not yet 21, in a round of visits, expeditions and conversations. From now on, Caroline was recording in her *Journal* her impressions of a near contemporary rather than of the friends of her father.

During his stay in Madeira, Sterling had met Dr. John Calvert, a fellow sufferer from tuberculosis and the two had become close friends and they planned to make a second visit to the island. As has been mentioned, stormy weather delayed their sailing, but it was no doubt the congenial and intellectually stimulating company of the Falmouth circle of Quakers and others that caused Sterling and also Calvert to spend the rest of the winter in Falmouth. Sterling describes the Fox families as follows:

Most worthy, respectable and highly cultivated people, with a great deal of money among them, who make the place pleasant to me. They are connected with all the large Quaker circle, the Gurneys, Frys, etc., and also with Buxton the Abolitionist. It is droll to hear them talking of all the common topics of science, literature and life, and in the midst of it: 'Does thou know Wordsworth?' or, 'Did thou see the Coronation?' or 'Will thou take some refreshment?' They are very kind and pleasant people to know.[42]

Caroline's contact with John Sterling during the years 1840 to 1844 was not continuous, yet a reading of her *Journal* convinces us that in this period John Sterling became the all-pervading influence and preoccupation in her life. Indeed the extracts from her *Journal* are fuller and more frequent than for any other part of her life, taking up almost half the total volume of the book. This was the period of the expansion of Caroline's personality, a period brimful of new experiences, new ideas, and a new understanding of the words of books and art. For Caroline it was the equivalent of a university education.

In the year 1840, John Sterling was in Falmouth from January to early April, living in lodgings and leaving his wife and young children in Clifton. During this time he was a frequent visitor at the Foxes home and there were many walks; one undertaken in a violent snowstorm, another 'a nice blowing walk',[43] sometimes they went geologizing, sometimes scrambling; on another occasion they spent the time wandering among the rocks 'on a day made for basking'.[44] In July of that year the Fox family stayed in Clifton and saw much of John Sterling, who guided them round Bristol Cathedral and took them to see the casts of Greek sculptures in the Bristol Institution.

The following winter John Sterling went to Torquay, but having been advised by his doctor that 'a quiet winter in Cornwall with his family would be vastly better for him than the intoxication of Italy',[45] he was back in Falmouth in April and determined to settle there. He found a house and Caroline and Anna Maria helped him with advice on choosing wall-papers and on the position of cupboards; they also worked in the garden at 'Sterling Castle'. When his wife Susan and the children arrived, visits were paid to their new home and there were outings to the seashore, where on one occasion they 'lounged on the beach most peacefully'[46]

In Julius Hare's memoir there is an account of his life at Falmouth contributed by one 'who knew him there intimately'; this well might have been Caroline herself.

> He used to rise as early as five o'clock, to read and write in his little study, overlooking the sea, spent much of the mornings in long rides and walks, in the keenest enjoyment of the life and beauty

around him, and returned to an early dinner with his children, entering into all their amusements, as if he were one of them. Christmas eve was always a gala day, when the task of ornamenting and illuminating the Christmas tree devolved principally on him. His sympathies were ever ready for small as well as great things; and the feelings of a child he always treated with respect. In the evenings he would often invite a few friends to join their happy little family party. We looked over his portfolios of German and Italian engravings, listening to his reminiscences of Italy, or to his sparkling thoughts on the great men whose portraits lay before us, or to his criticisms on the works and minds of the great artists. Sometimes these evenings were devoted to the reading of manuscript poetry,—sometimes to Wordsworth, his comments on whom were invaluable, full of light and love,—sometimes to an essay on Dante; but always to something that might help the young forward, whom he wished to regard him as an elder brother, ever ready to assist them in their difficulties, to give them faithful advice, and to exercise his many gifts as talents entrusted to him for their benefit'.[47]

Caroline saw John Sterling frequently during the rest of the year 1841. In April, 1842, he went by sea to Italy for about three months. Caroline saw him in London on his return in June of that year and with others they went to see the Temple Church and 'visited the grand old Templars, all lying in state under a shed waiting for readjustment';[48] another day they met John Sterling at Bridgewater House and saw the pictures there under his guidance. When John Sterling was back in Falmouth, walks and visits were resumed and there is mention of an expedition by boat: 'Floated in the harbour with the Sterlings, a very calm, thoughtful, and merry opportunity, as fancy led us'.[49]

At every meeting there was talk, wide-ranging, fascinating talk, on almost every literary and philosophical subject imaginable, all carefully noted down by Caroline. Sterling was well read in German literature and philosophy and seems to have aroused Caroline's interest in these subjects. It may have been from this time also that on John Sterling's recommendation, Caroline began reading Luther's version of the Bible in the original German. John Sterling described English authors he had known, such as Coleridge and Carlyle and talked about Shelley, Byron and Wordsworth. Then he talked about Italy and Italian painters, Raphael, Michael Angelo and Corregio; the last-named he admired above all others. Sterling gave his views on politics, on the corn laws, on India, and on the need for a British empire in Africa. He spoke on religion, Roman Catholicism, the Jesuits, and on Quakerism. There was speculative talk on the place of women in society, on mental difference between the sexes, on work and vocation, on self-scrutiny and on the weighing of motives. Very rarely does Caroline record her own views; occasionally she mentions a disagreement: for the period of these years 1840-43, her *Journal* is to a great extent a record of John Sterling's table-talk or rather his walking-talk, rather than of Caroline's own thoughts and feelings.

There are however here and there small indications of how Caroline felt towards John Sterling. During their first year of contact, Sterling was probably seen in the role of an elder brother and Caroline must have felt like an attentive, awe-struck, younger sister or indeed as a pupil. Her motto for 1840 was taken from the scene in Shakespeare's *Henry IV, part II* when Lady Percy speaks of her dead husband, Henry Hotspur.

> He was indeed the glass
> Wherein the noble youth did dress themselves.[50]

Caroline clearly saw herself as one of the youth who modelled themselves on their admired leader. Her few tributes to Sterling confirm this: 'Sterling was as usual our life. . . .'[51] 'Sterling came and walked with us to Pennance Cave on a day as brilliant as his own imagination.'[52]

Two years later she has this restrained comment: 'Sterling is truly an invaluable person to consult on any literary or logical difficulties, and his ready friendship seems really rejoiced to be able to help any who desire it in earnest'.[53]

During the years of their contact their relationship must have become a more equal one. Caroline recommended books for John Sterling to read and introduced him to George Fox's *Journal*. John Sterling gave her autographs, including an autograph letter from Coleridge, presented her with an engraving of an ideal head by the sixteenth-century artist Benedetto Gennari, and later lent her a portfolio of engravings.

Nowhere in the *Journal* is there any suggestion of their relationship being other than one of 'ready friendship'. Both John Sterling and Caroline were serious, high-principled people and Caroline a loyal member of the Society of Friends. As long as John Sterling was married it is unlikely that there could have been any acknowledgement of there being any special feeling between them.

A tragedy altered this. The gales that Caroline feared were blowing up. In the beginning of 1843 Sterling attempted to help his servants in moving a heavy table and this brought on a serious haemorrhage. His wife Susan was expecting a child and a baby girl, her sixth child, was born at

Easter. Then a few days later Sterling received the news of the death of his mother. His wife, still suffering from the strain of childbirth, hearing the news, murmured, 'Poor old man,' thinking of John's father. Two hours after she too was dead.[54]

Caroline's *Journal* makes no mention of this event and is silent about the growth of a closer more personal relationship between herself and John Sterling that must have followed it. For this intense period of Caroline's life we are dependent upon other sources, her brother Barclay's *Journal,* family tradition mentioned by a cousin, Violet Holdsworth, and also those revealing mottoes.

John Sterling was left a widower with six small children, he himself also being in poor health from his illness. Inevitably he turned to his friends, the Fox family, friends 'whose kindness is beyond all price, all description'.[55] Anna Maria and Caroline would have given both solace and practical help. In May of that year a letter to Barclay who had just returned from a tour of the continent told 'how the girls have suffered from their close and active sympathy with the bereaved husband, and assiduous care of the children. Poor C. [Caroline] has been recruiting at Wadebridge'.[56] At this juncture John Sterling and Caroline must have realized that their intellectual companionship could become a partnership for life or for what was left of life for John Sterling.

We do not know when he asked Caroline to marry him, nor for how long they considered themselves engaged. According to Violet Holdsworth, Caroline and John Sterling became engaged "very soon after his wife's death'.[57]

We have some information about the sequence of events. In June 1843 Sterling moved his family to Ventnor in the Isle of Wight, to a house close to his brother, Anthony. He revisited Falmouth in early July and accompanied the Fox family to the Friends Meeting. It is unlikely that John Sterling would have asked Caroline to marry him in May before his removal to Ventnor, as such a proposal would have come less than two months after his wife's death. It is possible that there could have been some conversation between the two at the time of his visit in July which could have led to thoughts, maybe unspoken, of an eventual engagement.

The actual proposal appears to have been made in January, 1844. Barclay's *Journal* records an exchange of letters between John Sterling and Caroline in that month. His entries are written in a code which may have satisfied his own need to preserve some secrecy, but would have provided but little obstacle to an inquisitive reader. Thus the entry for 21st January reads: 'Sgnilrit's rettel. Sc rewsna.' which can be translated as 'Sterling's letter. C's answer.' Then on the 28th Barclay writes: 'Poor C.: She bears up nobly but not without praying and stuggling'. On the 31st January John Sterling wrote his final letter to Caroline. The next day has the entry 'Scene – Poor C.'[58] This must have meant that the engagement was finally at an end.

According to Violet Holdsworth, who quotes from a letter to her mother she 'gave him up at the entreaty of her parents who disapproved of his views'.[59] Sterling's views were ones that he had reached through personal search and experience. In a letter to Julius Hare he had written:

> Christian truth is that and only that doctrine which commends itself to the minds of all who share in the Spirit of Christ, which spirit may be briefly described as a prevailing temper of reverential and affectionate self-denial. Taking all ages and countries through, the essential doctrine will be found to resolve itself into acknowledgement of Christ as the Ideal Man and therefore the representative of the Divine Mind towards us.[60]

Such a formulation of faith would commend itself to many Quakers of the twentieth century, but in Caroline's day it fell short of an open acceptance of the divinity of Christ. In the words of Violet Holdsworth 'he and she did love each other, but he was not sound in his beliefs so they could not marry'.[60] Another impediment to their marriage must have been the knowledge that as Sterling was not a Quaker their marriage would have had to be celebrated elsewhere than in a Quaker meeting and this would have lead to disownment from the Society of Friends.

Caroline's motto for 1844 may well have been chosen during those painful days of decision. She inscribed at the top of her page one line from Shelley's poem, *Adonais*, his lament written on hearing of the death of John Keats. It comes from stanza 32 and reads as follows:

> A pard-like spirit, beautiful and swift.[61]

This line could safely be written and even printed in the published version, even if it were seen as a tribute to John Sterling, as it reveals but little of Caroline's feelings. However when it is placed in its context and the words that follow are read, then Caroline's secret is open to all. Here are the words:

> A love in desolation masked.

The implicit meaning of the motto for 1844 must be an avowal by Caroline both of her love for John Sterling and also of her misery at the enforced ending of the engagement. The two lines from *Adonais* were no doubt in Caroline's mind, because for her the end of her engagement and the departure of John Sterling must have seemed like a death; to the outside world both her love and her sorrow had to be masked. From Barclay's *Journal* we learn that Caroline became ill with a cough and irritation which lingered on for several months.

But John Sterling was more gravely ill; he became gradually weaker and on 18th September, 1844, he died of the illness which had afflicted him all his life. Caroline had suffered the first and greatest tragedy in her life. She had expected gales before she dropped anchor and this was the first.

CHAPTER VI

The Lords of Humankind Pass By, 1840-44

DURING THE SAME PERIOD of time that Caroline's friendship with John Sterling was growing, she was brought into contact with several of the leading literary and intellectual figures of her day. Her motto for the year 1841 was one line from Oliver Goldsmith's poem *The Traveller*: 'I see the lords of humankind pass by'.[62] She did not include the line that precedes it 'Pride in their port, defiance in their eye', as this would not have been a true picture of the impression that these 'lords' made upon Caroline; but the line that follows the one chosen could with advantage have been included also: 'Intent on high designs, a thoughtful band'. This was indeed a true description of those she met at this time.

Up to the time that she met with John Sterling, the characters mentioned in her *Journal* were either scientist friends of her father or unusual travellers visiting Falmouth. During these years from 21 to 25 she met and talked with thoughtful men of high designs, people of such outstanding intellect who would have been unlikely to have talked seriously to a young girl unless there had been something brilliant or attractive about her also. Sterling has left no description of Caroline, but we do have two witnesses to the brilliance and dynamic personality of Caroline and of her brother and sister. The first account is by Thomas Hodgkin, later to marry, Lucy Fox, Caroline's first cousin and to become a noted amateur historian.

> I think that it was in the year 1843, probably in the midst of visits to Hare, Carlyle and Maurice, that they came to Tottenham to visit my father, who had recently married their second cousin Anna Backhouse, as his second wife. I remember how we children, brought up in the calm, sedate atmosphere of Tottenham

Quakerism, were astonished by the vivacious, sparkling talk of these Cornish Cousins.[63]

The second is by Maria Rogers, who became a close friend and here describes her meetings first with the Fox family and then with Caroline.

The next glimpse of the Fox family was at Penrose, when one day Mr. and Mrs. Robert Fox, their cousin, Mrs. Robert Barclay, of Blackwell, and Anna Maria, arrived unexpectedly and lunched with us. Well do I remember their reception by my father and mother-in-law, and felt without any words that these were guests they 'delighted to honour'. After luncheon we went for a walk, and Anna Maria was my companion. The rapidity of her thoughts and words gave me a vivid impression of her eagerness, and I could quite understand how her industry and suggestiveness might have started the Falmouth Polytechnic. She filled my thought for many a day, and I tried to find out all I could about her from my husband's family, who had long known her; but the discussion would always end with, 'You *must* see Caroline,' who I found had enchanted the county by a sparkle and humour they did not expect to find under the quiet Quaker garb.

Another year we were guests at Grove Hill; our host and hostess there had left the Society of Friends, and become members of the Church of England; but they were clothed with the gentleness and charity, the refinement and culture, of their Quaker bringing up. We did not meet any Friends there; but at last, on the second day of that great county gathering at the Polytechnic, while speeches were being made on the platform, I came suddenly on a knot of Friends in the body of the hall, and stood face to face with *Caroline Fox!* She greeted me with the immediate acceptance she held ready for all who came to her, which made you feel she had opened wide the door and let you in, and was willing to make the very best of you. We were quickly in absorbing talk; her dark eyes flashing, her whole face eloquent with power and response; we were interrupted in the middle of a story I was telling her about a poor woman who was crazed. I said to her 'Never mind, I will write you the rest'. She looked rather doubtfully as she said, 'Thank thee,' as if she thought I must have more leisure than usual in this busy world to talk of writing to one I knew so little.[64]

After John Sterling, the first of 'the thoughtful band, intent on high designs' was John Stuart Mill. He was then aged 33 and after being educated by his father to become a child prodigy held an important post at India House, had been editor of *The London and Westminster Review* and wrote widely on philosophic and political subjects. Caroline depicts him as follows: 'He is a very uncommon-looking person – such acuteness and sensibility marked in his exquisitely chiselled countenance. . . . His voice is refinement itself, and his mode of expressing himself tallies with voice and countenance'.[65]

He came to Falmouth to be with his mother and two sisters Clara and Harriet, who were nursing their sick brother, Henry, who was dying of consumption. Caroline had become a friend of Clara and John Mill was a close friend of John Sterling, so it was natural that he should join their walks and expeditions. Caroline's *Journal* for the months from March to May 1840 gives extensive reports of Mill's talk and also a revealing glimpse of the relative styles of the two friends. 'Sterling was the chief speaker and John Mill would occasionally throw in an idea to clarify an involved theory or shed light on a profound abysmal one'.[66]

Sterling seems to have had a mind, brimming with information and some of his talk, as reported by Caroline, reads more like a lecture to a student, giving his views on literary trends and comparing and contrasting literary and philosphical ideas. Mill, on the other hand seems to have had a more reflective and probing mind and would examine and follow up trains of thought.

John Stuart Mill had read and admired John Woolman's *Journal* and wanted to know more about Quakerism. Much of what he had to say would have been welcomed by Caroline and must have influenced her own religious thought.

Caroline was impressed by Mill and spoke of his 'wonderfully keen, quiet eyes'[67] and 'a face of such exquisite refinement'.[68] Friendship developed. Mill promised her autographs and presented her with 'A Calender of Odours' giving a list of trees and flowers that fill the air with sweet odours from March to July. The friendship however did not develop further, presumably because John Mill had already formed an emotional and intellectual attachment to Harriet Taylor, a married woman, who became his wife after the death of her husband some years later.

When Caroline was in London for Yearly Meeting in May 1840, John Mill showed them the treasures of the museum at India House. That day and the next there was talk on national character, on Quakerism, on the nature of motives and manners in society, on truth in things false. 'We all went off together, John Mill . . . evolving his clear because profound truths . . . in a crystal stream, his spirit's native tongue.'[69]

In 1843 Mill sent Caroline a copy of his book, *A System of Logic*, with certain chapters marked which he hoped that Caroline would read. She read the chapter on 'Liberty and Necessity' and approved of it.

Then the friendship faded. Mill did not come to Falmouth again; the last record of a meeting with him in London was in 1846, but the references to him are less warm and less extensive. In the meantime Caroline's friendship with John Sterling had grown and in 1846 she was still suffering from his loss. 13 years later she read Mill's book *On Liberty* and in a letter to her friend Elizabeth Carne, summed up her feelings:

> I am reading that terrible book of John Mill's on Liberty, so clear, so calm, and cold: . . . He looks you through like a basilisk, relentless as fate. We knew him well at one time, and owe him much; I fear his remorseless logic has led him far since then. This book is dedicated to his wife's memory in a few most touching words. He is in many senses isolated, and must sometimes shiver with the cold.[70]

Thomas Carlyle appears in the pages of Caroline's *Journal* as a prophetic figure of the mould of Jeremiah; powerful, dogmatic, dyspeptic, bewailing contemporary ills and errors: indeed a lord of humankind, intent on high designs. Her first sight of him was in May 1840 when she attended two lectures by him on the 'Hero as Man of Letters' and the 'Hero as King' and she gave such full reports of the substance of the lectures that they contain passages not afterwards retained in the published book *Heroes and Hero-Worship*. Carlyle was then 45 and Caroline not yet 21. Carlyle's lectures made a striking impression upon Caroline and her admiration comes through in the vivid words she uses to present him.

> He is a tall, robust-looking man; rugged simplicity and indomitable strength are in his face, and such a glow of genius in it – not always smouldering there, but flashing from his beautiful grey eyes, from the remoteness of their deep setting under that massive brow. His manner is very quiet, but he speaks like one tremendously convinced of what he utters, and who had much – very much – in him that was quite unutterable, quite unfit to be uttered to the uninitiated ear . . .[71]

A few days later she with other members of the Fox family met Thomas and Jane Carlyle at the home of John Mill and Carlyle in response to his Quaker guests, spoke warmly of George Fox's *Journal*. The evening's conversation is not very fully reported, but the young Quaker visitors must have made a favourable impression upon Carlyle, as the following year, when her uncle and aunt Charles and Sarah Fox called on Carlyle, he ran after them to say, 'Give my love to your dear interesting nephew and nieces!' John Sterling explained that Carlyle 'liked their healthy mode of Quakerism, as the sort of thing with which he can sympathize more than any other.'[72] In his *Life of John Sterling*, Carlyle gave his view of the Foxes. 'The family had grave elders, bright cheery younger branches, men and women; truly amiable all, after their sort.'[73]

Caroline met Carlyle twice in 1842, while in London for Yearly Meeting and reports their conversation at length. In her accounts of these meetings, Caroline conveys a different quality of interchange between herself and Carlyle from that which obtained with either John Sterling or John Stuart Mill. With both of the latter she was to a great extent the listener and disciple; Carlyle's dogmatic and provocative manner frequently stimulated Caroline to express her own opinions when they conflicted with his. For instance on the subject of capital punishment, she tried to expose Carlyle's inconsistency in being opposed to capital punishment whilst still tolerating the use of war. This seemed to tickle the prophet, as Caroline notes Carlyle's laughs, 'famous fellows, hearty and bodily'.[74] On another occasion she tackled his despairing view of the world by asking him 'if there was a single institution existing which was as he would have it'.[75] She then went on to ask him about his early life, showing herself to be a very confident person for a young woman of 23. Carlyle took to her and there followed a correspondence between the two, some of it concerned with a Cornish miner, Michael Verran, described in a later paragraph and some of it consisting of gentle teasing of Caroline's saying 'thou' to him. By this time Carlyle felt he was sufficiently intimate with her to address her as 'Dear Caroline' or 'Dear Miss Caroline'.

Caroline and her family visited the Carlyles several times during the next five years, the last of these visits being in May 1847, when they again challenged his despairing views. 'We had such a string of tirades that it was natural to ask, "Who *has* ever done any good in the world?" – "Why, there was one George Fox; he did some little good".'[76] When Thomas Carlyle's *Life of John Sterling* appeared in 1851, Caroline was hurt by the interpretation given of Sterling's conduct. 'It is painful enough to see the memorial of his friend made the text for utterances and innuendoes from which one *knows* that he would now shrink even more than ever, and God alone can limit the mischief, But He can. That the book is often brilliant and beautiful, and more human-hearted than most of Carlyle's, will make it but the more read, however little the world may care for the subject of the memoir.'[77] The friendship then appears to have lapsed, until 16 years later, when they met in the south of France. Carlyle was then aged 71 and had just lost his wife. On this occasion Caroline commented, 'I am very glad to have seen him again after an interval of many, many years, though it makes one sad to think of him – his look and most of his talk were so dreary'.[78]

Caroline had found in Thomas Carlyle someone whose ideas she could challenge and call in question; she remained for a time at least on terms of close friendship with him. From this friendship Caroline must have grown in her own judgment and intellectual ability. But Carlyle had another influence upon her. As has been mentioned earlier, Caroline had already embarked upon work with the cottage people of the district, but Carlyle gave Caroline a further encouragement to concern herself in those less fortunate than herself. From his study in Chelsea, Carlyle heard of the heroism of the Cornish miner Michael Verran and succeeded in engaging Caroline in raising a fund to help him. The story is best told in Carlyle's own words as given in his *Life of John Sterling*.

> One other little event dwells with me, out of those Falmouth times, exact date now forgotten; a pleasant little matter, in which Sterling, and principally the Misses Fox, bright cheery young creatures, were concerned; which, for the sake of its human interest, is worth mention. In a certain Cornish mine, said the Newspapers duly specifying it, two miners deep down in the shaft were engaged putting in a shot for blasting: they had completed their affair, and were about to give the signal for being hoisted up, – one at a time was all their coadjutor at the top could manage, and the second was to kindle the match, and then mount with all speed. Now it chanced while they were both still below, one of them thought the match too long; tried to break it shorter, took a couple of stones, a flat and a sharp, to cut it shorter; did cut it of the due length, but, horrible to relate, kindled it at the same time, and both were still below! Both shouted vehemently to the coadjutor at the windlass, both sprang at the basket; the windlass man could not move it with them both. Here was a moment for poor miner Jack and miner Will! Instant horrible death hangs over both,—when Will generously resigns himself: 'Go aloft, Jack,' and sits down; 'away; in one minute I shall be in Heaven!' Jack bounds aloft, the explosion instantly follows, bruises his face as he looks over; he is safe above ground: and poor Will? Descending eagerly they find Will too, as if by miracle, buried under rocks which had arched themselves over him, and little injured: he too is brought up safe, and all ends joyfully, say the Newspapers.

> Such a piece of manful promptitude, and salutary human heroism, was worth investigating. It was investigated; found to be accurate

to the letter,— with this addition and explanation, that Will, an honest, ignorant good man, entirely given-up to Methodism, had been perfect in the 'faith of assurance', certain that *he* should get to Heaven if he died, certain that Jack would not, which had been the ground of his decision in that great moment;—for the rest, that he much wished to learn reading and writing, and find some way of life above ground instead of below. By aid of the Misses Fox and the rest of that family, a subscription was raised to this Methodist hero: he emerged into daylight with fifty pounds in his pocket; did strenuously try, for certain months, to learn reading and writing; found he could not learn those arts or either of them; took his money and bought cows with it, wedding at the same time some religious likely milkmaid; and is, last time I heard of him, a prosperous modest dairyman, thankful for the upper light and safety from the wrath to come. Sterling had some hand in this affair: but, as I said, it was the two young ladies of the family that mainly did it.[79]

Of the 'two young ladies', it seems from the *Journal* as if it was Caroline who took the chief part in corresponding with Carlyle about Michael Verran and in receiving and passing on subscriptions. A little over 12 months later in January, 1844, Carlyle included this paragraph in a letter to Caroline

By the by, ought not you, with your neat swift pen, to draw up, on a half sheet of paper, an exact narrative of this man's act of heroism – authentic, exact in every detail of it – and reposit it in some safe place for a memorial of the same? There is no more genuine use that the art of writing can be turned to than the like of this. Think of it.[80]

We do not know whether Caroline ever undertook such a task, but for us to-day, Michael Verran's act of heroism is given a small place in history by Carlyle's vivid narrative.

During the same period of her life, Caroline met William Wordsworth on two occasions. After the disappointment of finding him away when the family called at Rydal Mount in 1837, the next opportunity occurred five years later. The poet was staying in Hampstead, with Hannah Hoare, and her grandson Gurney Hoare, a cousin of the Foxes, took them to meet him. Wordsworth held forth on the beauty of the countryside; on feeling instructing seeing and on having sympathy with the past; he bewailed that the love of the beautiful was lost in notions of shallow utility. As with Carlyle, Caroline felt confident enough to intervene and question the great man. She instanced Charles Lamb's appreciation of London rather than the countryside; then she spoke of poets who gave a voice to their yearnings after the Ideal rather than the Actual and expressed the hope that there would be a reaction to the materialism of the age. Wordsworth must have been impressed by Caroline as was shown by his manner of parting. 'We took a truly affectionate leave; he held my hand in both of his for some time, which I consider a marked fact in my existence!'[81]

They met again in October, 1844, when they were in the Lake District, shortly after the death of John Sterling. This time Caroline records his talk, but makes no mention of anything that she may have said. Perhaps she was silent; she was suffering from the sadness of her loss. During the visit, Wordsworth learned the news of Sterling's death. 'Dead!' he exclaimed; 'that *is* a loss to his friends, his country, and his age. A man of such learning and piety!'[82] Later Caroline records some words he used in speaking of the wet morning, with the autumn landscape then coming out with perfect clearness. 'It is like the human heart emerging from sorrow, shone on by the grace of God.'[83] Caroline's own human heart was still wrapped in sorrow. She saw him again two days later when she says, 'The old man looks much aged; his manner is emphatic, almost peremptory, and his whole deportment is virtuous and didactic'.[84] Wordsworth lived another six years, but they did not meet again.

In June, 1842, Caroline met her cousin, Elizabeth Fry, who took her and others to Coldbath Fields Prison, 'the best of our Houses of Correction, though a severe one, as whipping and the treadmill are still allowed.[85] A few days later she was shown round Hanwell Mental Hospital, by Dr. Conolly, the Superintendent, who 'had introduced the system of non-coercion in its fullest sense'.[86]

The following year, when in Norfolk, they dined at the Buxtons and met Sir Thomas Fowell Buxton, the leader of the anti-slavery movement, 'who was capital now and then'.[87] They were also given an introduction to George Borrow, who had just written *The Bible in Spain,* a tall, ungainly, uncouth man, with great physical strength, a quick penetrating eye, a confident manner, and a disagreeable tone and pronunciation.[88] In each of these latter instances, Caroline says nothing of any contribution she may have made at these meetings. But during these years of her young womanhood, before she was yet 25, she had indeed seen some of the lords of humankind pass by.

CHAPTER VII

Desolation Masked, 1844-46

ON JOHN STERLING'S DEATH in September, 1844, desolation entered Caroline's life. It may indeed have come to her earlier, when, yielding to the pressure from her family she withdrew from their engagement to marry. In the printed edition of her *Journal* there is no direct mention of John Sterling's death at the time that it occurred, but a few weeks after his death there is an entry appearing only in the first edition of her printed *Journal*, which reveals her private preoccupations. She gives a brief record of a dream.

> October 1. – Last night, in a dream, we were looking at S. T. Coleridge's letter to Lamb, and I asked him what it meant? 'It means Life, my dear,' he said.[89]

The 'he' can only have been John Sterling. This entry was omitted from later editions of the *Journal*; presumably it revealed too much.

We can also discern her feelings from her mottoes, and from some other indirect sources. We have seen how her motto for 1844 had expressed her sense of loss at the rupture of her engagement to Sterling and also her distress at the concealment of her love for him. That for 1845, the year following his death, expresses her grief and desolation. She again found some lines from Shelley which expressed her mental state. This time she chose three lines from a stanza of his poem, *Lines written in dejection above Naples*. The complete verse from which Caroline took lines 3 to 5 is as follows:

> Yet now despair itself is mild
>   Even as the winds and waters are;
> I could lie down like a tired child,
>   And weep away the life of care
>   Which I have borne and yet must bear,

36

> Till death like sleep might steal on me
> And I might feel in the warm air
> My cheek grow cold and hear the sea
> Breathe o'er my dying brain its last monotony.

It is significant that Caroline turned to the poems of Shelley for solace, rather than to the words of any of the Quaker writers such as William Penn, who had written about the experience of bereavement. She had no doubt been introduced to Shelley's poems by Sterling, who had described Shelley as the complete master of impassioned feeling. Caroline must have felt that the mood both of *Adonais* and of *Lines written in dejection above Naples* expressed her state of feeling better than any other words she could find.

We have some confirmation of her state at this time from the sudden lack of entries in the printed edition of her *Journal*, there being only eight entries between January and June, 1845. Her editor explains this as follows: 'In the years 1844 and 1845 came a time of great sorrow, and a considerable blank occurs in the journals of these and some of the succeeding years; what she wrote at this time containing, save so far as is extracted, nothing but a most sacred record of great personal suffering and inward struggle'.[90] This passage occurs only in the first edition of the printed *Journal*; it was omitted from the second edition, as no doubt revealing too much of Caroline's inner feelings and in place there appeared a more general statement with no mention of any specific dates, stating that her records of personal suffering and inward struggle were far too sacred to be printed.

The entry in the *Dictionary of National Biography*, the relevant number of which appeared in 1889, written by Richard Garnett is even more explicit.

> [Sterling's] death in 1844 may not have been unconnected with the depression into which Caroline fell in that year, and which left its traces on all her subsequent life. From this time her diary becomes less copious and interesting, partly from comparative infrequency of remarkable acquaintances, partly from the interruptions occasioned by ill-health, but partly also from a lack of buoyancy and a comparative limitation and timidity of thought.[91]

When she was in London for Yearly Meeting in 1846, she went to Samuel Laurence's studio to be drawn and this drawing (reproduced in an etching by Herkomer on the cover of this volume) reveals the delicacy and sensitivity as well as the pensive sadness of her face. After this she went with her brother Barclay and no doubt the rest of the family for a tour of Switzerland. Caroline says that the object of the tour was to enable Barclay to grow fat, but it was just as likely also planned to provide a change of scene for Caroline. They were away during June and July and spent some time in Geneva, but apart from a mention of some meetings with a Swiss ecclesiastical historian and with some American ladies, we have little information about what they saw or did.

CHAPTER VIII

All Must be Earnest, 1847-55

CAROLINE'S MOTTO FOR 1848 consists of a verse from a hymn by the Victorian hymn writer Horatius Bonar.

> Our age is but the falling of a leaf,
>   A dropping tear,
> We have not time to sport away the hours:
> All must be earnest in a world like ours.[92]

Up to this time Caroline emerges from the pages of her *Journal* as an acute, observant, highly-intelligent, gifted blue-stocking, not at all a typical Quakeress of her time. Now after her loss and desolation, the last line of this hymn seems best to describe the next few years of Caroline's life.

The brilliant circle of intellectual and literary people living in or visiting Falmouth had dispersed or been cut off by death. On the young Henry Mill's death in 1840, the Mill family had returned to London. Sterling's friend John Calvert, who was said to have been attracted to Anna Maria, had died in 1842 and John Sterling himself in 1844. From this period, the visitors described or reported on in the *Journal* were largely those of an older generation. There is no further mention of walks and expeditions in the countryside with friends and contemporaries near her own age.

On her visits to London, Caroline entered a different circle of friends, people who were more earnest and serious about Christian belief and about the nature of the church universal and its responsibility for exemplifying an ideal fellowship and protesting against the injustice of the social conditions of the time.

The man who impressed her most was Frederick Denison Maurice, who was chaplain at Lincoln's Inn and also Professor of Theology at

King's College, London. He was later to become, despite himself, the leader of the Christian Socialists. She met and corresponded with Charles Kingsley, disciple of Maurice and more ardent Christian Socialist. She was also attracted to the de Bunsen family, an unusual cosmopolitan family, who were at the centre of a circle of serious people, concerned about the institution of the Church and the expression of Christian belief in practical service. Charles de Bunsen, known in England as Chevalier de Bunsen, married to Frances Waddington from Wales, was Prussian ambassador in London and strove to bring together the German Lutheran church and the Anglican Church.

Before going on to speak of her new acquaintances, we must try to understand something of Caroline's own religious faith. After her death, a paper was found in her desk, describing her religious struggles and discoveries. Characteristically, some of what is written is an account of the teaching of others, but some of her words seem to come from a deeper source of experience. The first entries set out her feelings when she was just 21 years of age. She had listened to John Calvert, speaking on the worthlessness of a merely traditional faith in the highest truths; she felt that hitherto she had been taking things of the highest importance too much for granted, without feeling their reality. Then in her own words:

> The first gleam of light, 'the first cold light of morning', which gave promise of day with its noontide glories, dawned on me one day at Meeting, when I had been meditating on my state in great depression. I seemed to hear the words articulated in my spirit, 'Live up to the light thou hast; and more will be granted thee'. Then I believed that God speaks to man by His Spirit. I strove to live a more Christian life, in unison with what I knew to be right, and looked for brighter days; not forgetting the blessings that are granted by prayer.

Then later she says '... the truth came before me with a clearness and consistency and brightness indescribably delightful; the *reasonableness* of some Christian doctrines which had before especially perplexed me, shone now as clear as noonday; and the thankfulness I felt for the blessed light that was granted was intense'.[93]

During these years of her early twenties, when in constant discussion with John Stuart Mill and John Sterling, she could not help but be influenced by their religious and philosophical ideas. Either as a result of selection on the part of Caroline or on her editor's, the views of each of them quoted in the *Journal* are those that in some way confirm her own belief in the immediacy of personal experience. Thus in 1840 she gives these words of Mill: 'Avoid all that you prove by experience or intuition to be wrong, and you are safe; especially avoid the servile imitation of any other, be true to yourselves, find out your own individuality, and live and act in the circle around it' and later he says' . . . in the darkest passages of human existence a Pole Star may be discovered, if earnestly sought after, which will guide the wanderer into the effulgence of Light and Truth'.[94]

Two years after this she quotes a discussion which took place with John Sterling and this time gives her own words.

> Talked of our responsibility in the guidance of ourselves; of living in inward and outward consistency with such light as has dawned upon us; not attempting, like the foolish virgins, to walk by the lamps of any companions, however wise, if God has entrusted us with lamps of our own. On the entire self-sacrifice which is due to Truth: fearful is the wrench which must be endured in the separation from every form of falsehood, but if you can stand this, glorious will be the reward in Light and confidence of spirit. Sad and perplexing is the search, and often vain, for the wisest man of your time, whom you may joyfully accept as a leader. 'But,' I ventured to say, 'rather than this harassing search amongst the multitude of conflicting rays which show but an infinite number of tiny light-beams, would it not be wiser, in simplicity and faith, to direct the earnest gaze upward, where all rays of light converge in one glorious focus, and inward, if one ray is permitted to shine there to guide the teachable spirit through this misty, half-developed chaos of a world?'[95]

In her *Journal* for January, 1846, she writes down a statement of her faith. 'I have assumed a name to-day for my religious principles – Quaker-Catholicism – having direct spiritual teaching for its distinctive dogma, yet recognizing the high worth of all other forms of Faith; a system, in the sense of inclusion, not exclusion; an appreciation of the universal, and various teachings of the Spirit, through the faculties given us, or independent of them.'[96] We might see this as Caroline's attempt to weave together her own Quaker upbringing with the ideas she had received from Mill and Sterling.

Caroline, we may assume, was a regular attender at Quaker Meetings for Worship, probably twice on Sundays and once during the week. In the printed edition of the *Journal*, Horace Pym excluded nearly all references to Meetings for Worship, but Caroline Stephen must have seen the original journals before they were destroyed and in her article gives us some of Caroline Fox's comments. This observation is undated: 'Our

Meetings, I think, are more "lively" and weighty than sometimes; I trust there is a growing dread of the *form* of silence. . . .'[97] She records her mother's ministry and occasionally comments on it. 'Dearest mother spoke on "Whatsoever thy hand findeth to do, do it with thy might"; pointing out that our only might is in the strong Spirit of God, which will surely enable us to do whatever He requires at our hands; and if we neglect the little things, we assuredly fall by little and little. She told justly enough how our mock modesty, fear to injure a good cause by our advocacy, and so on, often hinder a work given us to do. My dear mother, surely thou art sharp with thy dagger!'[98]

In 1848 she records a generous tribute to a Quaker of the older generation.

> *May* 8.—Old Samuel Rundall has ended his weary pilgrimage, with his old wife sitting by his side: 'he departed as one who was glad of the opportunity'. He, far more than any I have seen, carries one back centuries in the history of opinion and feeling. He was a perfect Quaker of the old George Fox stamp, ponderous, uncompromising, slow, uninfluenced by the views of others, intensely one-sided, with all the strength and weakness of that characteristic; a man to excite universal esteem, but no enthusiasm; simple and childlike in his daily habits, solemn and massive in his ministry; that large voice seemed retained to cry with ceaseless iteration, 'The Kingdom of God is within you'. Last of the Puritans, fare thee well! There was a certain Johnsonian grandeur about him, and one would have lost much insight into a bygone time and an obsolete generation by not having known him.[99]

Caroline never became well-known as spiritual leader within the Society of Friends. Her name does not appear as either an Elder or as an Overseer, but during this period of her life she must have been more active in the concerns of the Society, as in 1853 for the first time we find her appointed as a representative of women Friends of Cornwall Quarterly Meeting to London Yearly Meeting.

The clearest statement that we have of her views on the Society of Friends in her time is contained in a letter she wrote to Charles Kingsley, dated just 'March 23rd'; the year was probably 1854 and if so the letter would have been written soon after her first meeting with him. It is worth giving almost in full.

So thou hast discovered a very truth, that we are neither a literary nor a theological little section of the Church – the 'inner life' amongst our worthies is I think as, or more, legible in their outward existence as in their most earnest writings – they don't conceive themselves, as expounding any new discoveries, or experiences but as simply taking our Lord's declarations & precepts de serieux & translating *them* – however imperfectly – into Life – Thus though we do not abound in striking writers, there are I believe very many amongst us who accept the commands 'Love your enemies' – 'Swear not at all' etc., as well as those of distinctly spiritual character, in as absolute a sense as the Church of Rome receives 'Take eat – this is my body – and my blood', 'Wash one another's feet, as I have given you an example' etc. – we seem just to reverse their order of taking the words spiritually & literally – but in either case where the act is an act of faith & love & loyalty, God's blessing is surely bestowed.

Well I don't know whether I've made out a case for my People on the ground of their being simple and practical believers rather than Artists in spiritual regions – but I shall leave it to thy kindest construction.[100]

Caroline did not consider herself to be an artist in spiritual regions. In a letter written on her birthday eight years later she says 'Ah, no, I have uncommonly little of the mystic element of meditation and communion in me'.[101] Her religion had to satisfy both her intellect and her feelings and it had to find expression in her life. At this stage her religious strivings previously satisfied by the open and free enquiry and self-examination of Mill and Sterling were met by the fervent prophetic vision of Frederick Denison Maurice that the Church could become the witness on earth of the purpose of God and a guide both to the individual and to society. For Caroline, the de Bunsen family may have provided her with an actual example of how to combine intellectual interests and practical service.

There were links of a personal kind with both Maurice and the de Bunsens. Frederick Maurice had married Anne Barton, the sister of Susan Barton, the wife of John Sterling, who had died tragically in childbirth. Ernest de Bunsen, the second son of the Chevalier de Bunsen had married Caroline's second cousin, Elizabeth Gurney.

John Sterling had been an admirer and disciple of Frederick Maurice, and Caroline first met Frederick Maurice and his wife in 1842 before Sterling's death. She had probably already heard of, or possibly read, his first major theological work published in 1838, entitled *The Kingdom of*

Christ; or, Hints on the Principles, Ordinances, and Constitution of the Catholic Church; In Letters to a member of the Society of Friends. In this book Maurice expresses admiration for George Fox's attempt to establish a universal kingdom of Christ, composed of those who felt led by the Holy Spirit. However he goes on to point out how the Society of Friends of his day had failed to achieve this ideal by their attention to outward formulas of faith, such as their peculiarities of dress and speech and also by their admission to membership of Quaker children who may not have consciously recognized the Light.

At her first meeting with Frederick Maurice, Caroline may have expected to find a critic of the Society, but she records 'he is not at all dogmatic in his manner, but kind and conciliating'.[102]

She saw him again several times four years later and Maurice took them to see the chapel with the beautiful windows and the new dining hall at Lincoln's Inn, where he was the chaplain. In 1849 she attended a lecture on theology by him at Queen's College and mentioned his 'quiet depth and loving compassionate soul'.[103] In the same year she and Maurice had a discussion on war and peace which she reported as follows:

> Stumbled somehow on War. 'Won't the world some day come to think with us?' quoth I. 'They will come to think rightly,' was his reply, 'no doubt, but perhaps very differently to you or I.' 'But would any nation dare to attack another which resolves under no circumstances to do them anything but kindness?' 'Well, I find that whenever I am most right, I may always expect to be most bullied, and this, I suppose, will go on; it brings home to one very strongly the meaning of the words, "Woe unto you when all men shall speak well of you".'[104]

In a letter to her friend Elizabeth Carne in 1852 she quoted with approval his teaching on living in the Truth. 'F. D. Maurice . . . helps each to feel how momentous and how fruitful is the Truth – it may be hidden, yet still living – in that form of Religion which you profess; and he points out how, by living earnestly in *it*, it expands and deepens, and by assimilating with other Truths, displaces gradually all that is incompatible with it.'[105] Caroline must have felt that Maurice's expression of faith confirmed the one she had written down six years earlier which she had named Quaker-Catholicism.

A few years previously John Sterling had introduced her to the writings of the German philosopher and theologian Schleiermacher and had encouraged her to translate some of his sermons. Caroline thought about attempting this task, but we do not know whether she began any work on it. After meeting Maurice she wrote to him in 1848 to ask for his advice on this plan. He replied counselling caution in the enterprise and saying 'the simple and affectionate discourses you propose to translate should I think be accompanied with some introduction, explaining from what very different points the Englishman and the German start'.[106]

Caroline was also impressed by Maurice's practical application of his Christianity through the foundation of the Working Men's College, which she called the 'People's College' and by the promotion of Working Men's Associations. She attended the Associated Trades' Tea at St. Martin's Hall in 1851 and expressed her views as follows: 'In listening to the workmen's speeches . . . we could not help feeling very thankful that such fiery spirits had been brought under such high and holy influences, leading them to apprehend self-sacrifice as the vital principle on which all successful co-operation must be founded'.[107]

Her meetings with the de Bunsen family must also have set her mind towards practical Christianity. Ernest and Elizabeth de Bunsen had been married just a year, when Caroline first met them in August, 1846. She and Anna Maria had breakfast with them and Caroline found them 'both so bright, merry, and affectionate'.[108] They became personal friends and they met both in London and in Falmouth. In 1847 at the time of Yearly Meeting, Ernest and Elizabeth accompanied them to an evening Meeting for Worship and afterwards 'He sang us some old German hymns. The rich sustained quality of his voice, and its wonderfully beautiful tones, were a rare treat to listen to. He seldom sings without accompaniment, and never unless he feels secure of sympathy, for it is a most serious, full-hearted affair with him – he cannot sing for show'.[109] Four years later Caroline and Anna Maria visited them at Abbey Lodge, their pretty house in Regent's Park and in 1857 Ernest de Bunsen visited them twice in Falmouth. Caroline was impressed by his talk and again charmed by his singing.

Relations with the Chevalier de Bunsen and his wife were also friendly, but there was a difference in generation and Caroline's *Journal* conveys to us the feelings of admiration and respect that she had for the older man. The Fox family were taken by Ernest to breakfast with his parents at Carlton Terrace and Caroline described the Chevalier de Bunsen as follows:

> The Chevalier has far more real beauty than I expected, exquisite chiselling about the mouth and chin, large grey eyes, a certain vagueness and dreaminess, but also a general decision of character in the expression of the face, and a fine glow of genial feeling over all.[110]

In 1851, at a dinner at Ernest's house, Caroline found herself seated next to the Chevalier at dinner. On this occasion he spoke pointedly and evidently with some knowledge about Quakerism.

> Your Society of Friends has done much good, and its Founders have said many admirable things, but it wants vitality. I am very fond of them, but I must speak the truth as I find it. Your great peril is an idolatry of the form of formlessness, instead of trusting the Living Spirit. But you are of vast practical importance, and will still do much if you will but keep clear of the traditional spirit of the age.[111]

On several occasions the Chevalier talked about the German Hospital in Dalston, where the patients were cared for by nurses who were deaconesses from Kaiserswerth in Germany. Pastor Fliedner, the founder of the Kaiserswerth community, had originally been inspired by Elizabeth Fry to open a refuge for prisoners. Later he added a school, a training college, and a hospital, all served by dedicated deaconesses. In 1850 Florence Nightingale had visited Kaiserswerth and in turn had received inspiration for her work of hospital reform. Caroline must have expressed particular interest in the hospital at Dalston as during their stay in London in 1849 they were taken to visit it.

> After dinner we went with the Bunsens to the German Hospital, and were charmed with the order, cleanliness, and comfort of the whole establishment, but above all with the dear Sisters from Kaiserswerth who are active in ministry here by night and by day. One of them, in particular might have sat to Fra Angelico, so seraphic was her face; it told of a heart perfectly devoted, and perfectly happy in its devotion.[112]

Through her meetings in London with Frederick Denison Maurice and with the Chevalier de Bunsen, Caroline had met with examples of the practical expression of Christian faith, Maurice's Working Men's College and de Bunsen's German Hospital. These must have given her fresh inspiration for the educational and charitable work which she and Anna Maria did in Falmouth. These were her teaching in the infants school, her visiting of old people in her district, her work in the Sailors' Home and her support for the Royal Cornwall Polytechnic.

We do not know how much teaching Caroline did in the Infant School, nor how much satisfaction she obtained from it. With her quick, incisive mind, she could have been a formidable teacher. The following two extracts reveal both her sharp dagger and also by contrast her feeling of compassion for the children.

> January 12 [1844] Finished my week's work at the Infant School, and wrote in the Visitors' Report Book, that as many eminent men were very stupid at school, there was every hope for the sixty-three there.[113]
>
> February 18 [1846]. At the Infant School, by way of realizing a lecture on affection and gratitude to parents, I asked each of the little dears what one thing they had done for their mothers that morning? and I confess it was really humbling, as well as instructive, to discover that one of the tiny young creatures had washed some pocket handkerchiefs, another lighted the fire, another helped to lay out breakfast things, another washed the baby's cap, whilst most of them had taken part in tending the baby whilst mother was busy.[114]

Of her visiting of old people in the cottages there has been mention earlier. Here she describes one of her experiences in December 1853 'And sitting down under the hedge, old Pascoe and I read of Christian and Hopeful passing over the River, and we looked across to the cottage of one who had long been trembling on its banks, but had now been carried over, and welcomed by the Shining Ones.'[115]

She was a supporter and visitor of the Royal Cornwall Sailors' Home and in 1853 she befriended a Prussian sailor, called Kisting, of whom she gives this account:

> We have just had a long visit from a Prussian sailor-friend of ours from the Sailors' Home, called Kisting: he is a ship's carpenter, who fell from the mast and broke a leg and hand, but is now nicely mended. He is quite a man of education, and is delighted to have books; moreover, we have taught him to read as well as talk a little English during his dreary confinement, and I was excessively charmed at receiving a lovely, graceful little note from his sister, thanking us for the small kindnesses shown to him. He is thoroughly with *us* in thinking the manufacture of war machines 'unnatural and unchristian,' and he said when he saw two cannons taken on board ship, with great circumstance, and heard the clergy pronouncing their blessings on them, 'I felt that it was not right.' . . .[116]

Some years later she spoke of her friendship with another sailor, which led to her writing an account of his reclamation, but this will be mentioned when it occurs.

She was an active supporter of the Royal Cornwall Polytechnic Society in Falmouth, which the Fox family had established and financially supported. It was founded in 1833 and its stated object was to 'promote the useful and the fine arts, to encourage industry, and to elicit the ingenuity of a community distinguished for its mechanical skill'. It contained a library and a museum. Lectures were given in the evening and an annual exhibition of arts and handicrafts was held, when prizes were awarded. According to family tradition the idea for the Polytechnic originated with Anna Maria, when only 17 and the name was chosen by Caroline herself before the word 'Polytechnic' had come into common use. This tradition has received confirmation from the volume of Caroline's *Journal* recently brought to light. The entry for 17th April 1833, when she was not yet 14 reads: 'Anna Maria has founded a society to which I have given the name of Falmouth Polytechnic Society and collected more than 4£.'[117]

Many of the lecturers at the Polytechnic were guests of the Fox family. In 1841 John Sterling gave the inaugural lecture of a winter series on 'The Worth of Knowledge'; later he spoke on the characters of the Greek, Roman and Italian heroes, artists and writers, whose plaster busts were to be awarded as prizes to those who had won merit in the Arts Exhibition. In 1852 Caroline wrote of an occasion as follows:

> We are in the thick of a very pleasant Polytechnic. The Art Exhibition is better, they say, than in any previous year; nevertheless, they have not hesitated to give Anna Maria two bronze medals – one for a wave in the Bay of Biscay, the other for her Lisbon Sketch-Book; and moreover, a public compliment was paid them, which I am almost apt to fancy well deserved.[118]

These years from 1847 to 1855 were certainly more serious ones than those that were filled with friendship with Mill and Sterling, but they were also full ones. They might be summed up by the words Caroline wrote in her *Journal* on 18th March, 1848. 'Plenty to do and plenty to love, and plenty to pity. No one need die of ennui.'[119]

But we must not leave this period of her life without recording a dramatic incident that could have brought her injury or death. This was Caroline's encounter with a bull. Here is the incident in her own words:

> *March* 10 (1853). – As we turned the corner of a lane during our walk, a man and a bull came in sight; the former crying out, 'Ladies, save yourselves as you can!' the latter scudding onwards slowly but furiously. I jumped aside on a little hedge, but thought

the depth below rather too great – about nine or ten feet; but the man cried 'Jump!' and I jumped. To the horror of all, the bull jumped after me. My fall stunned me, so that I knew nothing of my terrible neighbour, whose deep autograph may be now seen quite close to my little one. He thought me dead, and only gazed without any attempt at touching me, though pacing round, pawing and snorting, and thus we were for about twenty minutes. The man, a kind soul but no hero, stood on the hedge above, charging me from time to time not to move. Indeed, my first recollection is of his friendly voice. And so I lay still, wondering how much was reality and how much dream; and when I tried to think of my situation, I pronounced it too dreadful to be true, and certainly a dream. Then I contemplated a drop of blood and a lump of mud, which looked very real indeed, and I thought it very imprudent in any man to make me lie in a pool – it would surely give me rheumatism. I longed to peep at the bull, but was afraid to venture on such a movement. Then I thought, I shall probably be killed in a few minutes, how is it that I am not taking it more solemnly? I tried to do so, seeking rather for preparation for death than restoration to life. Then I checked myself with the thought, It's only a dream, so it's really quite profane to treat it in this way; and so I went on oscillating. There was, however, a rest in the dear will of God which I love to remember; also a sense of the simplicity of my condition – nothing to do to involve others in suffering, only to endure what was laid upon me. To me the time did not seem nearly so long as they say it was: at length the drover, having found some bullocks, drove them into the field, and my bull, after a good deal of hesitation, went off to his own species. Then they have a laugh at me that I stayed to pick up some oranges I had dropped before taking the man's hand and being pulled up the hedge; but in all this I acted as a somnambulist, with only fitful gleams of consciousness and memory.[120]

Dearest A. M. joined me, and we walked homewards and met the carriage with poor dear mamma in it to be scared by the ill-looking object called her daughter.... But it was long before I could thank God meetly for his immense goodness to me.[121]

The members of her family responded to this emergency in characteristically different ways. Anna Maria who had been a terrified witness of the whole scene, prayed that her sister might be spared this awful death and cried out inwardly that she would never grudge her if Caroline was taken later on. Her brother Barclay wrote a poem, which does not survive well into this century, but contained the lines:

> God of mercies! When I think
> How she lay upon the brink
> Of an agonising death![122]

Her mother at Meeting for Worship on the following Wednesday spoke in the meeting gathering her thoughts round the text 'What shall I render unto the Lord for all his benefits towards me?'[123]

The owner of the bull, Sir Richard Vyvan, wrote a letter of deep apology which contained the lines 'Had the humblest pauper been exposed to the hazard which you have undergone, I should have been deeply grieved. Judge then of my mortification and *horror* that you should have been in peril of your life on this occasion'.[124]

CHAPTER IX

Dim with Childish Tears, 1855-60

DURING THE FIVE YEARS FROM 1855 to 1860, Caroline suffered the loss of three members of her family, her brother Barclay, her mother, and then her brother's widow, Jane. For the year 1859, a few months after her mother's death, she chose the following lines from Wordsworth's poem, *The Fountain*.

> My eyes are dim with childish tears,
>   My heart is idly stirred,
> For the same sound is in my ears
>   Which in those days I heard.[125]

as her motto for the year. They seem also appropriate for this period of recurring losses.

Her brother, Barclay, had become engaged to Jane Backhouse, in March, 1844, a few weeks after the time that Caroline's own engagement had been broken off. Jane Backhouse came from a strict Quaker family and wore the plain dress of Quakers. Maria Rogers, a friend of Caroline's met her in the following year and described her in these words, 'Mrs. Barclay Fox was a beautiful woman; the costume became her; I was struck with the intelligent glowing expressiveness of her face, which gave great charm to everything she said'.[126]

When Caroline was visiting the Carlyles in May 1844 she told them of Barclay's engagement and he sardonically commented: 'Well, they must club together all the good sense they've got between them; that's the way, I suppose'.[127] They were married in October, 1844, and settled at Perran Cottage, near Falmouth, and over the next 11 years five children were born.

Barclay's health however gave cause for anxiety. It seems likely that he too suffered from the consumption that had attacked so many of their friends. In 1853 he and Jane went abroad for his health while the children were looked after by other members of the family. Anna Maria and Caroline had the care of little Gurney aged 3 and Caroline writes about him as follows:

> Jane has all her children in the North except little Gurney, who is my heart's delight, and a perfect mass of sunshine to us. I have never before had a child thrown so much on my care, and most delicious I find the tender little dependence. And then I have also the very new and very exalting experience of my presence or absence being absolutely a matter of importance to one dear human being.[128]

In November, 1854, at a time when grim battles were being fought in the Crimea, Barclay went abroad again, this time to Egypt. Caroline went to Southampton to see him off and describes it in these words.

> But besides this, Robin and I have been with Barclay to Southampton, and seen him off for Alexandria in the good ship *Indus*, and then with heavy hearts went to London. Everything on board the *Indus* looked promising; the second officer magnificently gave up his luxurious cabin, and when the bell rang we left our Brother, feeling that we ought to be thankful for the present and trustful for the future. His brother-in-law, John Hodgkin, came down that morning from London to see him off; he was in every way a great comfort and strength, for we had a little time of solemn silence and as solemn prayer before going on board, which, though most touching, was essentially strengthening and helpful. The weather has been so fine since he left that we feel we have had no pretext for anxiety, and all we hear and all we know argues that he is doing the very wisest thing possible, and that there is every probability of its bringing him into a very different state of health from that in which we part from him. And how different from an embarkation for Sebastopol![129]

His first letters were cheerful; then in April, 1855, came the tragic and unexpected news of his sudden death from a haemorrhage of the lungs. Barclay had always been close to his two sisters. Caroline wrote of him in these words, 'He was always the joy of our life, and there was always the most perfect mutuality of feeling and interest. I do not mean, of course, that we always agreed in opinion; but we were always sure of each other's hearts'.[130] Her sad feeling of loss comes across in her *Journal:* 'April 26. – I could fill volumes with remembrances and personal historiettes of interesting people, but for whom shall I record them now?'[131] Her friend, Maria Rogers, described the effect upon Caroline.

For a few days she was very poorly, and allowed to be quiet and alone in her own room. . . . When she left her room again her letters were full of watchfulness and sympathy for those around her – of herself she spoke not – and last week I had a letter in much of her former tone, as though she had come back, and, most naturally, to daylight and the day's work.[132]

At this time Caroline was able to provide comfort to Barclay's widow, Jane, and Jane's letters to Caroline at the time were said to have 'had a tenderness and soothed tone in them kept for her alone'.[133]

After this her mother's health began to fail and Anna Maria and Caroline devoted themselves to her care.

But all was not sombre. In May, 1856, Maria Fox's state of health must have been sufficiently reassuring to allow Caroline and some other members of the family to attend Yearly Meeting and to combine it with a round of sight-seeing in London and a visit to Oxford on the way back. This is how Caroline describes it to her friend Elizabeth Carne:

Penjerrick, June 27.—What can I tell of our London interests? The Yearly Meetings? No, that thou wouldst be sure to treat profanely. The luminous fountain at the Pantechnicon? Well, it was very beautiful, leaping up to the top of the dome, and being flooded from thence with colour. The Nineveh Marbles? We saw them, in a very edifying manner, under the convoy of Edward Oldfield, who made the old life live again for us with marvellous vividness and authenticity. And the Print Room, containing also the drawings of the old master, Cellini's beautiful vase, and Albert Dürer's marvellous carving. Oh! and the Peace fireworks and illuminations, which I saw so well from the top of our friend's house, and which were indeed excitingly beautiful. Or the blaze of azalias and rhododendrons at Bury Hill? Or Tupper, the Proverbial Philosopher? from whom I heard neither Philosophy nor Proverb; the Coleridges, and Christabel's birthday fête? a picturesque garden party around her June-pole? Or Oxford? where we spent a few glorious hours, subdued, overawed by the sense of age and nationality which seems to fill the place. Professor Maskelyne did the honours charmingly; and Merton, and Magdalene, the Bodleian, the Radcliffe, the Clarendon, the Theatre, the shaded cloisters and the beautiful gardens, all leave such an impression on the memory and imagination as I should feel much the poorer for lacking. And then they are building a wonderful Museum, with a glass Gothic dome or roof, and one or two hundred pillars of British marbles interspersed amongst the masonry. They have

> beautiful red serpentine, but not the green; would it be very difficult or expensive to supply them with one? I was delighted to hear of their successful experiment to unite Town and Gown by a Working Man's College; about two hundred Town students have now mustered, and a capital staff of collegians are delighted to teach them. They talk of one for the women too, but ladies are not numerous at Oxford. . . . Fare-thee-well, good Queen Bess. With much love from Penjerrick to Penzance, thy ever affectionate,— C. F.[134]

The following year she accompanied her father to the British Association Meeting held in Dublin. Robert Were Fox read a paper to the Geological Section on the temperature in mines. They attended the Viceroy's reception at Dublin Castle and Caroline had this comment to make on it:

> Naturally it was the gayest scene I have ever been in, but the Viceroy was so good-natured, and there were so many interesting people to chat with, that after the first solemnities of presentation it was a very pleasant evening. Of course not so pleasant as a home one over reading and drawing; but still very pleasant as things go.[135]

She met Dr. Livingstone back from his expedition to the Niger and admired his earnest simplicity and his quiet fun.

But in 1858 Maria Fox's life was drawing to its close. In her account of Caroline Fox in the *Friends' Quarterly Examiner*, Caroline Stephen gives the last stages of Maria's illness from the unpublished parts of Caroline Fox's *Journal*. They speak of her great thankfulness for the life she had had and her confidence in a future life beyond death. Caroline writes of her mother seeing death as a change of houses, a step onwards and of her feeling that the veil separating her from heaven had become thin. Her words to-day strike us as being limited by the conventional imagery of her time, but we can still feel the intensity of feeling behind them. Maria Fox died in June 1858.

Speaking of her loss, Caroline says 'The sense of loss deepens, but we don't know its compass yet. But I must add that the sense of peace continues to be nearer than that of loss. . . . Our days pass cheerfully, and they are so full of things to be done that I yearn for more of stillness and silence that we might realize a little more where we are and where she is'.[136]

The family spent the spring of 1859 in Italy, chiefly in Rome and in Naples. It was the very eve of the first great advances towards the unification of Italy. That winter Garibaldi had been recruiting followers for his irregular corps which was to operate in the mountains and lakes of northern Italy. Caroline makes no mention of these matters, but their leaving Italy may have been hastened by the rumours of preparation for war.

On the way back they spent some time at Cannes, which they enjoyed. Here they met the de Bunsen family again and on the 5th March in celebration of Madame de Bunsen's birthday, they had an expedition to la Napoule and the massif de l'Estérel. Writing some years later Caroline recalled 'the aroma of white heath . . . and the views opening all the way up and the dear Estrelles coming out in all their loveliness in a framework of pine'. In another such letter she wrote about the occasion, 'We passed the house and terrace where we dined that bright day and listened to the loving speeches – the old Baron made one about G. Fox and liberty of conscience in drinking our healths'.[137] It is possible also that it was during this stay in Italy that Anna Maria made contact with the Protestant schools in Naples and in Turin, which soon became one of her major preoccupations.

When Caroline got back she wrote in her *Journal*:

> June 5.—Settled once more into dear, beautiful home-life, the near and distant memories being all so living and precious beyond all words. The welcomes from dear home friends, rich and poor, have been truly heart-warming, and it is delightful to be able right honestly to rejoice with them in being home once more.[138]

But there was another family tragedy. Barclay's widow, Jane Fox, seems also to have been affected by the prevalent consumption. On account of her health, she went with her children to the south of France in May, 1860, and there at Pau the illness recurred and she gradually became weaker and suddenly died. Caroline and her father and Anna Maria were summoned out of the Friends Quarterly Meeting to be told the news of Jane's illness and left immediately for France, arriving after her death. In a letter of the time, Caroline gives a vivid picture of their stay in the Pyrenees.

> What a sweet and true and welcome note from thee followed us from Pau to Pierrefitte a day or two since, and how truly our hearts responded to it. You have heard no doubt abundantly about us and our darling children, and I am thankful to say that I can still confirm the good account of them. Henry is quite well again, and the others are nicely, and all very, very dear; they enjoy the loving letters of sympathy which they and we receive, and their hearts are

very open to any such expressions. They talk most easily and naturally of their mother, and love to do so, and have various precious little gifts, which proved to be parting ones, to treasure for ever. They have liked the mountain life we have been living together, and are thorough boys at climbing and snow-balls, and dear George has been sketching industriously and with a great deal of taste. Three are now drawing at this table with Aunt Annie as I write, and dear Robert reading to us; really you would think us a cosy-looking party in a pretty bright *salon* this quiet evening. Grandpapa is in one of the great chairs by the fire, and Gurney and Jane are very busy with him and a baby squirrel, which the landlady of Pierrefitte gave them this morning. Grandpapa looks so benignant and happy with these three young creatures playing over him. Sometimes it seems so wonderful that such a tempest can have passed over them, and yet they look so unscathed; but such is their Heavenly Father's gracious arrangement for His weak, young creatures. Robert, of course, has much more maturity than the others, feeling more deeply and silently, and bearing it bravely. Our time at Pierrefitte answered well: a comfortable hotel in a quiet village at the head of a beautiful valley, and at the base of a glorious group of snowy mountains, range upon range, and all so beautiful. There were such ravines to explore, such mountain torrents and waterfalls to admire, such lovely wildflowers to collect—gentianellas, cowslips, hepaticas—and it is pretty to see little Jane's loving life amongst the flowers. We have been collecting cowslip roots to plant by her mother's grave, because she enjoyed them so exceedingly. We hope to have Saturday to spend at Pau and see that things are arranged as we should like, and to plant some little memorials of our love. Then on Monday we hope to proceed homewards, and arrive by the end of the week. Robert is bravely wishing to be there, and to meet all that has to be met in such a return as it must be to a headless home. Still, how little can any of them realise the immensity of their loss; how well it is that they cannot.[139]

The death of Jane brought about a great change in the lives of Anna Maria and Caroline. They became the guardians of the four orphan boys, Robert, George, Henry and Gurney, aged 14, 13, 11 and 9.

The only daughter, Jane, aged 7, went to live with her maternal uncle and aunt, Edmund and Juliet Backhouse. Caroline writes of her enjoyment of her new role as follows:

We have had a lovely week or two together at Penjerrick, and I don't know what we should do now without our darling boys. Surely this spring of heart towards them is a token for good. . . . The boys seem to fill a great deal of our life. Oh, the cravings for due qualification for wider responsibility. . . . Another good, full, busy, happy week has coursed along at such a pace.[140]

From that time forward Anna Maria and Caroline became inseparable. Their friends always thought of them and talked of them as one blended personality. On a headland above Falmouth Bay there stood in their day two tall chimney stacks which were given the nicknames of Anna Maria and Caroline. In the time when crinolines were fashionable, Anna Maria and Caroline wore the straight dresses of Quakeresses, standing out like chimney stacks among the wearers of crinolines.

Later in that year 1860 the Fox family received a visit from Alfred Tennyson and his friend Francis Palgrave. Caroline draws this picture of the former:

Tennyson is a grand specimen of a man, with a magnificent head set on his shoulders like the capital of a mighty pillar. His hair is long and wavy, and covers a massive head. He wears a beard and moustache, which one begrudges as hiding so much of that firm, powerful but finely chiselled mouth. His eyes are large and grey, and open wide when a subject interests him; they are well shaded by the noble brow, with its strong lines of thought and suffering.

A few days later Holman Hunt and Val Prinsep called and Caroline gives this contrasting picture of the former, 'a very genial, young-looking creature, with a large, square, yellow beard, clear blue laughing eyes, a nose with a merry little upward turn in it, dimples in the cheek, and the whole expression sunny and full of simple boyish happiness'.[141]

When her brother Barclay had died five years previously, Caroline in despair had asked for whom she could then record her historiettes of interesting people, yet these pen pictures show that she had recovered some of her former skill. But these were almost the last that we find in her printed *Journal*.

CHAPTER X

To Lose that Health, 1861-71

IN THE LAST TEN YEARS of her life, Caroline's circle of friends and acquaintances contracted. Few intellectual or literary figures are mentioned in her *Journal* and there seem to have been no further visits to London for Yearly Meetings.

The explanation lies in the state of her health. So many of her friends and family had died from consumption, Henry Mill, John Calvert, John Sterling, Barclay Fox, Jane Fox, that it would have been surprising if Caroline had escaped untouched. Indeed in 1843 she suffered from a haemorrhage which she described as follows:

> After dinner I was writing to Aunt Charles, and on running upstairs for more paper, I was startled to find myself spitting blood. It proved to be only from the throat, but I, for half an hour, took it entirely as a signal of death, and shall, I believe, often look back with satisfaction to the solemn quietness which I felt at that time. I finished Aunt Charles's note, and then lay down alone, and felt altogether rather idle about life, and much disposed to be thankful, or at any rate entirely submissive, whatever might be the result.[142]

There was a further haemorrhage in 1848 and in January, 1850, she chose as her motto for the year these lines

> To lose these years which worthier thoughts require,
> To lose that health which should those thoughts inspire.[143]

After the death of her mother, Caroline's health further declined and in Caroline Stephen's words '*she* then became the chief solicitude for her father and sister'.[144]

During these last 10 years of her life, Caroline's letters to her cousin, Lucy Hodgkin, are composed largely of family news, visits, illnesses, deaths, but there are many references to the four nephews who had become the joint responsibility of Anna Maria and herself. They seem to have attended boarding schools: there is a mention of an occasion when Gurney was returning to school by train and his carriage caught fire and there was considerable alarm before the train was stopped. But they spent their holidays with Caroline and Anna Maria, usually at Penjerrick. We hear of them in 1861 sedulously attending lectures at the Royal Cornwall Polytechnic; but we also hear of more normal recreations. In November 1861, Caroline writes, 'My father and the Boys have been high busy producing fresh ponds and a fountain which are at length pronounced a great success. It is all very pretty, but to me the best part of it is the pleasure and amusement it has been giving to the constructors'.[145] Two years later she writes: 'The boys are going on delightfully, they have developed a passion for housebuilding of late strong enough to drag them out of bed betimes of a morning'.[146] In December of 1863 we hear of them taking part in a capital charade.

But the boys grew up quickly. Robert, the eldest, started work at the age of 18 and at 22 he married a fellow Quaker, Ellen Bassett, in the Friends Meeting House at Leighton Buzzard and they set up house in Falmouth.

Eighteen months later a baby girl was born and Caroline gained some of the satisfactions and delights of being a grandmother by adoption. Writing to Lucy Hodgkin she says: 'The sight of Ellen's rapturous absorbing happiness with her little Lilian gives me a delightful sense of what I trust lies but a little way before thee and Robert has his full share in this baby enthusiasm and is a very successful but rather original nurse'.[147]

George at 18 went off for a trip to South Africa, bringing back Cape bulbs for the garden at Penjerrick, and paid a second visit a few years later. At 23 he became engaged to Mary Wake, not a member of the Society of Friends. Caroline however took to her and in almost her last letter of her life wrote, 'She is so simple, gentle and affectionate and has such quiet ladylike ways that it is most easy to love her'.[148]

Henry, who seems to have been delicate and reserved, was apparently Caroline's favourite. When the boys went to stay with Thomas and Lucy Hodgkin in Northumberland, Caroline wrote 'If you don't like Henry particularly, I'll never forgive you'.[149] She did not need to fear. The Hodgkins took to Henry and he came to live with them and was found a place in a bank. In 1868 when he was 19, Caroline wrote about a visit that Henry paid to Falmouth. 'We are *delighting* in him; his outward vigour and manhood, his inward thought and tenderness: and spite of his appendages of beard and moustache his likeness to his father comes out to us far more clearly than it ever did before and is a constant luxury.'[150]

He later found work in London and shared lodgings with Jonathan Hodgkin (Thomas Hodgkin's half-brother), where 'he was supremely happy'.

The youngest of the four nephews, Gurney, appears to have been high-spirited, sociable and athletic. In 1870 we hear of him playing in a great cricket match with Truro. He too left Falmouth and went to live and presumably work in Pinchenthorpe, Yorkshire and then moved to lodgings in Newcastle.

In the hope of relieving Caroline's recurrent bronchitis several journeys were taken abroad in search of milder climates. We have some information about two of these journeys. One of them was an unexpected one for Caroline to take. In May, 1863, she travelled with a delegation to Spain who had gone there in order to plead for the release of a number of Spanish Protestants who had been imprisoned for preaching their faith. The attention of Quakers had been drawn to these Protestants in faith and name by a report in the Quaker periodical, *The Friend*, then a monthly. This had led to a steady interest and collections were made to provide support for their families while they were awaiting trial and to meet the cost of their defence. The most prominent of the Spanish Protestants was Manuel Matamoros, the son of an army officer, who discovered he had religious scruples about serving in the army. He visited Gibraltar, met with Protestants there and experienced a religious conversion. He returned to Spain and began preaching in Barcelona and in Granada. He was arrested, imprisoned in Granada pending his trial and then found guilty of attempting to abolish or change the religion of the state and sentenced to eight years imprisonment, which could have been served in the galleys. The World Protestant Alliance took the matter up and a petition was sent to Queen Isabella of Spain, requesting his pardon. This was followed by the formation of an international deputation with representatives from 10 countries, which travelled to Madrid to ask the Queen personally for the pardon. Robert Were Fox was a member of the delegation and Caroline and Anna Maria accompanied him. The Queen of Spain commuted the sentence of imprisonment to one of exile. Matamoros was brought out of Spain and found a new home amongst other Spaniards, in Oran under French government in North Africa. Caroline wrote of the expedition to her friend Elisabeth Carne in light-hearted vein.

> *Blois, June 6.*—This Spanish frisk has been most memorable; the great object of the journey accomplished far beyond their hopes, though in a way to save the Queen's pride and their vanity. Many think that it is a first and very important step in the direction of

religious liberty, from which they will not dare to recede with all Europe looking on, and speaking its mind very distinctly.

We saw a good deal of some very thoughtful and liberal-minded Spaniards, but it is sad to see in what a state of timidity and unmanliness some of the really superior ones are kept by the narrow laws of their country. I wonder what has become of all the *ci-devant* prisoners? Have you got them in England? I hope not. They would be in worse peril there than in the prisons of Granada. Anna Maria and I contrived to get a great deal of common-place enjoyment out of the excursion, whilst our betters were engaged in conference with their brother deputies. They were a gallant set of men, representing ten different nations, and we felt very proud of them.[151]

They travelled home in a leisurely manner and spent some days in the Pyrenees. Caroline described it as follows:

The Pyrenees looked so inviting that S. Gurney and our party scudded off to them for a couple of most glorious days in the neighbourhood of the 2 Bagnieres. The mountains were most condescending and the huge Maladetta and Pic du Midi and crowds of others rewarded our ascents by the grandest clearest visions.[152]

In the autumn of 1866 the family went to Italy and to southern France. They visited Venice and in November were at Hyères on the French riviera. They also took with them the family pet marmozet, Johnny. Caroline makes Johnny the writer of a letter from Hyères which contains this passage, 'You will be glad to hear that this climate suits my health as well as that of my family. I like to sit with them upon the cistuses and myrtles and look out on the sea from under the pines, and draw a little, and make friends with the people'.[153]

In February they were at Cannes and Caroline wrote:

We are close to the sea and A.M. [Anna Maria] bathes with enthusiasm before breakfast. Yesterday was her birthday and we spent it at beautiful Napoul amongst the Estrelles where sea and sky mountains trees rocks joining with any amount of white heath and flowering shrubs made it all as fascinating as possible. And then the snowy Alps came out in their majesty and it was very hard to leave them....[154]

Caroline had set her heart on Anna Maria having the same birthday treat as Madame de Bunsen had had seven years previously. Of another expedition she wrote, 'We stopped on the way to gather flowers in a wonderful plain, brilliant with anemones, white red lilac and purple.'[154]

In March they were in Mentone and Caroline described a walk they had with a Friend, James Tuke. 'He took us a lovely walk up the valley yesterday where the banks were all alive with beauty, and cloud topped and snowy mountains frowned down upon us and the green and golden sea smiled.'[155]

At Mentone, Caroline renewed her acquaintance with Thomas Carlyle, then a sad widower in poor health. Caroline describes their stay there as follows:

> The manifold beauty of this place bewitches us, and we are able to take long excursions on donkeys amongst the mountains and quaintest of mountain villages.... We had a picnic at Roccabruna, in the olive grove behind that grotesque place, in honour of nice little Tuke's birthday. It was a brilliant scene, with all the bright children flitting about in the sunshine.[156]

At home in Falmouth there was her work at the Royal Cornwall Sailors' Home down by the harbour and her visiting of old people in the district. Caroline and Anna Maria evidently made regular visits to the Home and to the Infirmary attached to it to see any sick or distressed sailors admitted to the Home from ships calling at the port: they read to them or prayed with them.

We have fuller information about two sailors whom Caroline particularly befriended. The first was a Scots sailor who was brought into the hospital from an American ship. Her letter of 28th November, 1862, to Julia Sterling describes her feelings for him.

> *November* 28.—Thou shalt rejoice with me over my poor Scotchman at the Sailors' Home. (My romances are so apt to centre there!) Well, he was brought in several weeks ago, frightfully ill and suffering; a very perilous operation might possibly have relieved him, but they dared not attempt it here, and wanted to send him to a London hospital. He earnestly desired to be left here to die quietly, and I own I was very glad when at last they let him have his way, as it seemed very probable that the operation would be fatal. Well, somehow, we formed a very close friendship. He had frightened away the good people (the clergyman, &c.) by his stormy language, when really he was half delirious from agony; but we were nearer the same level, and so, as I said, we formed a romantic friendship. He poured out the story of his life, which had separated him from all his friends for more than twenty years. 'Oh! I was a bad, bad, bad boy! My life has been one course of sin!' and

he was utterly hopeless of forgiveness. Oh! the fixed despair of those poor eyes. I urged him to allow me to write to his family to tell of his contrition and ask forgiveness; but he said it was impossible that they could forgive him; the prodigal had wasted *his own* share of his father's heritage, but he had wasted theirs, and then ran away from them to America, and broke their hearts. What he would give to fall down before his father and beseech his forgiveness; but it was all too late. He cried bitterly, but for a week or two he would not let me make the attempt, which he was certain was utterly useless. He was evidently sinking, and I felt so strongly that if it were possible to win the forgiveness of his family, he would then be able to believe in a higher forgiveness; so last Sunday I wheedled his father's address out of him, and got his tacit consent to my letter going, though he was certain there would be no one there to receive it. The thought of my Scotchman haunted me to-day, so in I went and found a most loving letter from his brother hailing him as alive from the dead; I ran down to the Sailors' Home and found another from his sister in ecstasy of joy, and telling of his father's complete forgiveness and tender love. 'He would have spent his last shilling to come to you, but he is gone!' Oh, I have never seen anything more exquisitely touching than the floods of wonder and ecstacy when I took in my treasures. It was still an almost incredible joy; he poured forth his thankfulness and his tears before God, to think that he had still brothers and sisters who forgave him, and loved him, and received him as alive from the dead. His father he had felt certain was dead, so that was no shock, but to think how his love had clung to him to the last! Now I believe he will find no difficulty in believing in that Higher Love which has already done such great things for him! He covered his sister's letter with kisses, saying, 'It's my sister's heart, her heart'. She had telegraphed to a soldier brother near Chatham to come to him at once, so two or three may possibly be with him in a few days! I hope that all this joy will not have killed him before they come, but I should think it must hasten the end. I did not leave him till he was quieter, and I have since been writing most happy letters to them both. There, my dear, is a long story for thee, but I could not help telling thee what has made me quite tipsy. Excuse my happiness, and believe me, thy   C. F.[157]

    Caroline was so impressed by the Scots sailor's response to her and by the softening and change in his character that she wrote a short account of his reclamation. It is a small leaflet of four pages entitled *The Wanderer's Return* and was printed at The Orphans' Printing Press, Leominster.

From this we learn that, feeling his end near he asked for the prayer of Jesus in the Gospel of John, chapter 17 to be read to him; his condition worsened and he died a few days before Christmas.

The second sailor hailed from Liverpool and was admitted to the Sailors' Home, ill and destitute. He recovered and during 1864 and 1865 wrote an account of his life at sea called *A Sailor's Story*. It was written in pencil on sundry copy books and was edited by 'a friend' who selected quotations to head the chapters. This friend was probably Caroline, but the work must have been completed by Anna Maria, as the story concludes, 'Since this narrative has been written one of the ladies to whom I am especially indebted has been called away to Heaven – very vividly near me does her kind presence often seem, urging me to a more devoted faithfulness in the Master's service'. This certainly refers to Caroline. It is possible that this sailor is identical with the one mentioned in a letter of May 9th (attributed to the year 1863) addressed to Lucy Hodgkin where Caroline speaks of her 'dear quondam sailor boy, Edwin Allen, who was all but dead with dysentery, but improved wonderfully on having to change to another room'.[158] *A Sailor's Story* is a vivid and convincing account of continuous adventures at sea, both in merchant ships and in the navy and includes several escapes from shipwreck, becoming ice-bound a whole winter in the arctic sea and being marooned on an uninhabited island. The writer tells of being present at the annexation of Aden, whaling in the antarctic, gold-digging in Australia and in America and the illegal shipping of slaves to Brazil. The character that emerges is of a robust, courageous, hard-drinking, good-hearted man, loyal to his mates, unawed by authority, an attractive dare-devil.

She continued with her work of visiting old people in her district and with her Bible class. About the former we have this little extract from a diary kept by a cousin, Mariana Tuckett:

> November 21st 1858—Yesterday morning Caroline and I went to visit a number of poor people. . . . At one cottage a woman was bad with a cold and in the last day or two a rash had come out. Caroline sent me away and then the woman showed her arm covered with great white bumps, strongly suggesting small pox.[159]

Of the Bible Class we have an extract from her *Journal* quoted by Caroline Stephen, 'My Friday old women and I are so happy. I invited them to sing one week, and now they beg that they may pray too. By all means let us be refreshed together'.[160] After her death one of her addresses to a Bible Class was printed in *The Friends Quarterly Examiner* for 1872. It is a simple unaffected account of the lives of Old Testament prophets and others who had experienced a form of conversion.

Then there was the Friends Italian Schools Fund, which became a principal concern of Anna Maria, but Caroline must have been involved too. The freedom of thought and speech, which followed upon the liberation of nearly the whole of Italy by 1861 allowed the small Protestant Church in Italy, the Waldensians, the opportunity to preach and teach the Bible openly. In September of that year Garibaldi published an address to the women of Italy to awake them to the necessity of improving the moral and material conditions of the lower orders of their countrymen. It included these words as translated in the pages of *The Friend.*

> Political liberty does not suffice, they must partake of its benefits and attain that degree of education which alone can emancipate them from the degrading prejudices and ignorance which the corrupt portion of mankind has tried to keep them. . . . Let there be formed committees of ladies to assist the needy and to establish schools for their education.[161]

An Italian Ladies Philanthropic Association was formed chiefly to set up schools in Naples and in Palermo. In the north a Ladies Committee was set up in Turin and appealed for help to the ladies of England. The committee must have been Protestant in membership and inspiration as they took the opportunity to set up schools where the Bible in the Italian tongue could be taught.

Anna Maria Fox became the joint Honorary Secretary of a fund to collect subscriptions and transmit them to Turin for schools in Turin, Milan, Spezia and Naples. It became known as the Friends Italian Schools Fund and reports of the work done by the Italian committee were regularly given in *The Friend.* In 1862 the name of Caroline Fox appears as one of those to whom subscriptions could be sent.

When Garibaldi came to England in 1864, he visited Par in Cornwall, to see his former lieutenant, Colonel Peard. Caroline turned out to welcome him at the station and attended a reception given to him the next day. It would have been natural for Anna Maria or Caroline to have mentioned their work for the Ladies Committee in Turin, but Caroline does not mention this in her *Journal.*

Their concern for Protestant schools in Italy must have taken a strong hold upon the two sisters, for the two of them set about translating English religious tracts and stories into Italian. We have the names of six such booklets with titles including *The Power of the Word,* and also *The Cabin Boy Bob* and *Walter and Willie.* They were presumably printed to provide teaching material for the schools in Italy.[162]

Il Mozzo Bertino, the translation of *The Cabin Boy Bob,* was published in 1867. That same year a Friend at Yearly Meeting, Charles Wilson, said that he had been informed that there were numerous errors in the translations of Friends' tracts into Italian; indeed they 'contained absolute "nonsense" and would not be read'.[163] We do not know whether these were the tracts translated by Anna Maria and Caroline, as none of them seems to have survived. They are not mentioned in Caroline's *Journal*, nor in her unpublished letters to Lucy Hodgkin. We only know of their existence from a catalogue of books by Cornish authors, *Bibliotheca Cornubiensis*, by G. C. Boase and W. P. Courtney, published in 1874. It is possible that these were in fact the tracts criticized and that their scarcity and the absence of any mention of them was because Anna Maria and Caroline made sure that they were withdrawn from circulation and preferred to make no reference to them.

It is on a quiet note that Caroline's life drew to a close. 'During the Christmas of 1870, when the snow lay on the ground, with sunshine and blue skies overhead, she looked blooming, and walked frequently a mile or two to the cottages around; but when the thaw set in, her friends trembled for her; the damp chilly air never suited her, and it was a cause of distress to be cut off from out-of-doors objects of interest. She took cold when going her rounds with New Year gifts, and it quickly turned to a more severe attack of bronchitis than her lessening strength could struggle through; and although the sense of illness seemed lifted off, the old rallying power was gone.'[164] After two or three days illness she died in her sleep on 12th January, 1871.

The life of Caroline Fox would have filled a silent page of history, if it were not for the publication of those extracts from her *Journal* some 11 years after her death. In his desire for maintaining privacy, Horace Pym, the editor, made a selection which inevitably gives an incomplete picture of Caroline, presenting the social and public figure rather than allowing to emerge the contradictory facets of a human being.

I believe that this present study has enabled us to know her better; perhaps she has both grown in stature and also moved nearer to our own human scale. Still she keeps part of her personality concealed, unknown.

We carry away two conflicting pictures of Caroline Fox, difficult to reconcile; the first the eager, sparkling young girl, challenging the finest intellects of her day, the second the sad, quiet Quaker lady who seems to have lost her originality and power. We must conclude that the tragedy in her life was more painful and seering than anyone has previously acknowledged.

How do we appraise her now? I do not think that our growing acquaintance with Caroline Fox has altered her place in literature. She was above all a mirror to certain contemporary literary and public figures, a discerning psychologist who perpetuated their idiosyncracies on paper, a fluent chronicler of their words, a Boswell to many Johnsons. In the first part of her life her creative urge was concentrated in presenting her characters on the stage of her *Journal.*

Her life seems to fall into three phases, first the short but brilliant period in her early twenties; next the intense time of her love for John Sterling and the agony of having to give him up, his sudden death and her consequent depression; then the more sober period of her involvement in service to her neighbours in Falmouth. I think that we can see how the personal tragedies in her life gave her a greater depth of feeling and compassion for the sad and lonely. From her experience of loss, she could comfort the bereaved. Perhaps from her memory of her own attempt to break away from constricting conventions, she could reach an understanding of her wayward sailors. So we may remember Caroline Fox not only as the brilliant literary woman, but also as the hitherto unrecorded servant of the poor and sorrowful.

Bibliography and References

1. WRITINGS OF CAROLINE FOX

c. 1864   *The Wanderer's Return* (pamphlet), Orphans' Printing Press, Leominster, n.d.

1872   Bible Cases of Conversion (Written for a Bible Class), *Friends Quarterly Examiner,* 1872, 4th month, Vol. 6, No. XXII.

1882   *Memories of Old Friends*, being extracts from the *Journals and Letters of Caroline Fox of Penjerrick, Cornwall, from 1835 to 1871,* edited by Horace N. Pym. (Title on spine) *Caroline Fox her Journals and Letters.* London, Smith, Elder & Co., quarto 1882, octavo two volumes 1882, octavo one volume 1883. Republished 1972 as *The Journals of Caroline Fox, 1835-1871,* A Selection, edited by Wendy Monk, London, Elek.

2. WORK DONE JOINTLY WITH ANNA MARIA FOX

A. EDITING

1874   *A Sailor's Story,* An Autobiography. Anonymous, signed A— B—., Falmouth Hospital, 1864-65
London, Samuel Harris & Co., Penryn, John Gill & Son. N.D.

B. TRANSLATIONS INTO THE ITALIAN

1867   *Il Mozzo Bertino,* Racconto Vero, Florence, Tipografia Clandiana. Translation of *The Cabin Boy Bob,* Wesleyan Conference Religious Tracts, No. 101.

Undated   *Il Poter della Parola,* Florence. Transl. of *The Power of the Word, Memoirs of Pastor Von Maasdyk.*

Undated   *Che cosa uno puo fare,* London, Ferretti. Transl. of *What one man can do.*

Undated   *Il Poter della Fede,* Falmouth, Tregaskis, Transl. of *The Power of Faith.*

Undated   *Gualtiero & Gulielmo,* Naples. Transl. of *Walter and Willie.*

Undated   *Le due Percorelle,* Naples. Transl. of *The Two Lambs.*

3. Unpublished Sources

Letters to Sir Richard Owen and to Charles Kingsley, British Library, Department of Manuscripts, Add. MS. 39954, 42580, 41299.
Letters to Lucy A. Hodgkin, Thomas Hodgkin, Howard Fox, and others. In private hands.
Minute Books of Cornwall Quarterly Meeting, Women's Meeting, 1844-70, DD SF 20 & 21, Cornwall Record Office, Truro.

4. Published Sources

Allen, Peter, *The Cambridge Apostles,* The Early Years, C.U.P. 1978
The Annual Monitor for 1859. London, A. W. Bennett.
The Annual Monitor for 1872. London, F. B. Kitto & E. Marsh.
Boase, George Clement & Courtney, William Prideaux.
Bibliotheca Cornubiensis, Vol. 1 1874, Vol. 2 1878, Vol. 3 1882, London, Longman, Green, Reader & Dyer.
British Friend, 1867, Vol. 25, No. 6, p. 143.
Brett, R. L. (ed.) *Barclay Fox's Journal,* London, Bell & Hyman, 1979.
Carlyle, Thomas, *The Life of John Sterling,* London, Oxford University Press, World's Classics, 1933.
Collins, J. H., *A Catalogue of the Works of Robert Were Fox, F.R.S.,* chronologically arranged with notes and extracts and a Sketch of his Life, Truro, Lake & Lake, 1878
Crewdson, H. A. F. *George Fox of Tredrea and his three daughters, A Century of Family History,* Privately printed, 1979.
Delpech, Jacques, *The Oppression of Protestants in Spain,* London, Lutterworth Press, 1951.
Dictionary of National Biography, London, Smith, Elder & Co., Vol. 20, 1889, Caroline Fox, Charles Fox, Robert Were Fox. Vol. 54, 1898, John Sterling.
Fox, Charlotte, *Recollections of Our Old Home,* printed for private circulation, London, R. Barrett & Son, 1868.
Fox, Hubert (ed.), *Mariana's Diary,* Falmouth, Royal Cornwall Polytechnic Society. N.D.
(Fox, Samuel Middleton) A Grandson, *Two Homes,* Plymouth, William Brendon & Son, 1925.
The Friend, 1860-67.
Hankin, Christiana C., *Life of Mary Anne Schimmel-Penninck,* Vol. 2, Biographical Sketch and Letters, London, Longman.
Hare, Julius Charles, *Essays and Tales by John Sterling,* collected and edited with a memoir of his life. 2 Vols. London, John W. Parker, 1848.
Harris, Wilson, *Caroline Fox,* London, Constable, 1944.
Hodgkin, Thomas, Memories of old Friends: Anna Maria Fox, *Friends Quarterly Examiner,* 1898, 1st month, No. 125.

Holdsworth, L. Violet, Cousin Caroline: Caroline Fox of Penjerrick from a kinswoman's point of view. *Friends Quarterly Examiner*, 1945 10th month. No. 316.

Hughey, John David, *Religious Freedom in Spain, Its Ebb and Flow*, London, Carey Kingsgate Press, 1955.

Maurice, Frederick, *Life of F. D. Maurice*, chiefly told in his own letters, 2 vols., London, MacMillan 1884.

Monk, Wendy, (ed). *The Journals of Caroline Fox*, 1835-1871, A Selection, London, Elek, 1972.

Packe, Michael St. John, *The Life of J. S. Mill*, London, Secker & Warburg 1954.

Stephen, Caroline, Caroline Fox and her family, Part 1 *Friends Quarterly Examiner*, 1882, 4th month, No. 62, Part 2. 7th month, No. 63.

The Times, Saturday, 18th February, 1978, Saved from the flames at Penjerric, R. L. Brett.

Tod, Robert, *Caroline Emelia Stephen, Quaker Mystic*, 1834-1909, privately published, Birmingham, Robert Tod. 1978.

Tuell, Anne Kimball, *John Sterling, A Representative Victorian*, New York, MacMillan for Wellesley College, 1941.

References and Notes

THE FIRST MENTION OF ANY REFERENCE gives the title of book and author, or title of article, author and name of periodical. Subsequent mention gives title only or an abbreviated title. Reference to *Memories of old Friends, Caroline Fox, her Journals and Letters* appear as *Journal*. Page numbers refer to the 1st edition. Full particulars of all published and unpublished sources are given in the Bibliography.

CHAPTER I. CAROLINE FOX

1. *Two Homes*, by A Grandson (Samuel Middleton Fox), p. 67.
2. *The Annual Monitor for 1872*, pp. 72-73.
3. See Bibliography, pp.68-70 for fuller particulars of the editions of the books mentioned.

CHAPTER II. BIRTH AND PARENTAGE

4. *Life of Mary Anne Schimmel-Penninck*, Hankin, Christiana C., Vol. 2, p. 114.
5. 'Memories of old Friends: Anna Maria Fox', Hodgkin, Thomas, *Friends Quarterly Examiner*, 1898, 1st month, No. 125, pp. 115-16.
6. 'Caroline Fox and her Family,' Stephen, Caroline, *Friends Quarterly Examiner*, 1882, Part 1, 4th month, No. 62, pp. 274-75.

REFERENCES AND NOTES

7. *Two Homes,* p. 47.
8. 'Caroline Fox and her Family,' *Friends Quarterly Examiner,* 1882, p. 283.
9. 'Caroline Fox and her Family,' *Friends Quarterly Examiner,* 1882, p. 282.
10. 'Caroline Fox and her Family,' *Friends Quarterly Examiner,* 1882, p. 275.

CHAPTER III. CHILDHOOD, 1819-35

11. *Journal,* p. xviii.
12. *Life of Mary Anne Schimmel-Penninck,* pp. 109-10.
13. *Barclay Fox's Journal,* Brett, R. L., (ed.) p. 34.
14. *The Times,* Saturday, 18th February, 1978, Saved from the Flames at Penjerric, Brett, R. L.
15 & 16. *The Times.*
17. *Two Homes,* p. 67.
18. *Journal,* pp. 190-91.

CHAPTER IV. CALM WATER, 1835-40

19. *Journal,* p. 50.
20. *A Catologue of the Works of Robert Were Fox,* Collins J. H., p. 20.
21. *Journal,* p. 14.
22. *Journal,* p. 15.
23. *Journal,* p. 51.
24. *Journal,* p. 37.
25. *Journal,* p. 35.
26. *Journal,* p. 1.
27. *Barclay Fox's Journal,* pp. 101-2.
28. *Journal,* p. 3.
29. *Journal,* p. 14.
30. *Journal,* p. 14
31. *Barclay Fox's Journal,* p. 251.
32. *Journal,* p. 18.
33. *Journal,* p. 19.

CHAPTER V. JOHN STERLING, 1840-44

34. *Journal,* p. 53.
35. *Essays and Tales by John Sterling,* Hare, Julius Charles, p. cxxxiii.
36. *The Life of John Sterling,* Carlyle, Thomas, O.U.P. Worlds Classics, p. 66.

37. *The Life of John Sterling*, pp. 108-9.
38. *The Life of John Sterling*, p. 202.
39. *Barclay Fox's Journal*, p. 225.
40. *The Life of John Sterling*, p. 132.
41. *Journal*, pp. 126-27.
42. *The Life of John Sterling*, pp. 206-7.
43. *Journal*, p. 58.
44. *Journal*, p. 62.
45. *Journal*, p. 103.
46. *Journal*, p. 136.
47. *Essays and Tales by John Sterling,* pp. clxix-clxx.
48. *Journal*, p. 165.
49. *Journal*, p. 171.
50. *Journal*, p. 50.
51. *Journal*, p. 63.
52. *Journal*, p. 65.
53. *Journal*, p. 171.
54. *Life of John Sterling*, p. 254.
55. *Life of John Sterling*, p. 257.
56. *Caroline Fox*, Harris, Wilson, p. 85.
57. *Cousin Caroline*: Caroline Fox of Penjerrick from a Kinswoman's point of view, *Friends Quarterly Examiner*, 1945, 10th month, p. 237.
58. *Barclay Fox's Journal*, pp. 367-68 and *Caroline Fox,* Harris Wilson, p. 86.
59. *Cousin Caroline*, p. 237.
60. *John Sterling*, Tuell, Anne Kimball, p. 348.
61. *Journal*, p. 187.

CHAPTER VI. THE LORDS OF HUMANKIND PASS BY

62. *Journal*, p. 115.
63. *Memories of old Friends*: Anna Maria Fox, p. 124.
64. *Caroline Fox and her Family*, pp. 296-97.
65. *Journal*, p. 69.
66. *Journal*, p. 73.
67. *Journal*, p. 85.
68. *Journal*, p. 88.
69. *Journal*, p. 106.
70. *Journal*, p. 322.

REFERENCES AND NOTES

71. *Journal*, pp. 95-96.
72. *Journal*, p. 128.
73. *Life of John Sterling*, p. 206.
74. *Journal*, p. 155.
75. *Journal*, p. 162.
76. *Journal*, p. 220.
77. *Journal*, p. 270.
78. *Journal*, p. 341.
79. *Life of John Sterling*, pp. 222-23.
80. *Journal*, p. 188.
81. *Journal*, p. 160.
82. *Journal*, p. 195.
83. *Journal*, p. 197.
84. *Journal*, p. 198.
85. *Journal*, p. 164.
86. *Journal*, p. 167.
87. *Journal*, p. 183.
88. *Journal*, p. 184.

CHAPTER VII. DESOLATION MASKED, 1844-46

89. *Journal*, p. 192.
90. *Journal*, pp. xxii-xxiii.
91. *Dictionary of National Biography*, Vol. 20, p. 91.

CHAPTER VIII. ALL MUST BE EARNEST, 1847-55

92. *Journal*, p. 228.
93. *Journal*, pp. xxi and xxii.
94. *Journal*, p. 74.
95. *Journal*, p. 172.
96. *Journal*, p. 204.
97. *Caroline Fox and her Family*, p. 408.
98. *Caroline Fox and her Family*, p. 402.
99. *Journal*, p. 230. The name is spelt Rundell in the later editions.
100. Unpublished letter to Charles Kingsley, British Library, Department of Manuscripts, Add MS. 41299.
101. *Caroline Fox and her Family*, p. 427.
102. *Journal*, p. 156.

103. *Journal*, p. 238.
104. *Journal*, p. 240.
105. *Journal*, pp. 282-83.
106. *Life of F. D. Maurice*, Maurice, Frederick, p. 454.
107. *Journal*, p. 269.
108. *Journal*, p. 210.
109. *Journal*, p. 216.
110. *Journal*, p. 217.
111. *Journal*, p. 266.
112. *Journal*, p. 239.
113. *Journal*, p. 187.
114. *Caroline Fox and her Family*, p. 408.
115. *Journal*, p. 292.
116. *Journal*, p. 285.
117. *The Times*, 18.2.1978.
118. *Journal*, p. 281.
119. *Journal*, p. 230.
120. *Journal*, pp. 286-87.
121. *Caroline Fox and her Family*, pp. 399-400.
122. *Journal*, p. xxiii.
123. *Caroline Fox and her Family*, p. 402.
124. *Caroline Fox*, Harris, Wilson, pp. 36-37.

CHAPTER IX.   DIM WITH CHILDISH TEARS, 1855-60

125. *Journal*, p. 319.
126. *Caroline Fox and her Family*, p. 296.
127. *Journal*, p. 189.
128. *Journal*, p. 291.
129. *Journal*, p. 298.
130. *Caroline Fox and her Family*, p. 298.
131. *Journal*, p. 302.
132. *Caroline Fox and her Family*, p. 405.
133. *Caroline Fox and her Family*, p. 298.
134. *Journal*, pp. 307-8.
135. *Journal*, p. 314.
136. *Caroline Fox and her Family*, p. 414.
137. Unpublished letters to Lucy A. Hodgkin, 3rd Feb. (?) 1868, 22nd February, 1867.

138. *Journal*, p. 319.
139. *Caroline Fox and her Family*, p. 418.
140. *Caroline Fox and her Family*, p. 420.
141. *Journal*, p. 325.

CHAPTER X. TO LOSE THAT HEALTH, 1861-71

142. *Journal*, p. 180.
143. *Journal*, p. 259.
144. *Caroline Fox and her Family*, p. 299.
145. Unpublished letter to Lucy A. Hodgkin, 14th November, 1861.
146. Unpublished letter to Lucy A. Hodgkin, 9th May, 1863.
147. Unpublished letter to Lucy A. Hodgkin, 19th March, 1869.
148. Unpublished letter to Lucy A. Hodgkin, January, 1871 (?).
149. Unpublished letter to Lucy A. Hodgkin, 18th September, 1867 (?).
150. Unpublished letter to Lucy A. Hodgkin, 19th June, 1868.
151. *Journal*, p. 333.
152. Unpublished letter to Lucy A. Hodgkin, 6th June, 1863.
153. *Journal*, p. 338.
154. Unpublished letter to Lucy A. Hodgkin, 22nd February, 1867.
155. Unpublished letter to Lucy A. Hodgkin, 7th March, 1867.
156. *Journal*, p. 341. (Spelling of Roccabruna corrected. In the first edition it is misspelt Roccabonna.)
157. *Journal*, pp. 331-32.
158. Unpublished letter to Lucy A. Hodgkin, 9th May, 1863 (?).
159. *Mariana's Diary*, Fox, Hubert (ed.), p. 19.
160. *Caroline Fox and her Family*, p. 421.
161. *The Friend*, 1861. 9th month, New Series, Vol 1, No. 9, pp. 233-34.
162. See list in Bibliography.
163. *British Friend*, 1867. 6th month, Vol. 25, No. 6, p. 143; *The Friend*, 1867, 7th month, Vol. 7, No. 78, p. 135.
164. *Journal*, pp. xxv-xxvi.

Index

ALFESTON, Stephen (French tutor), 9
BARCLAY, Maria, see Fox, Maria
Barclay, Rachel (maternal grandmother of C.F.), 6
Barclay, Robert (maternal grandfather of C.F.), 6
Barclay, Robert (author of *Apology*), 6
Beche, Sir Henry de la, 14-15
Borrow, George, 35
British Association for the Advancement of Science, 4, 17, 54
Bull, encounter with, 48-50
Bunsen, Charles de (Chevalier), 40, 43, 45-46, 55
Bunsen, Ernest de, 43, 45-46
Buxton, Sir Thomas Fowell, 22, 35

CALVERT, Dr. John, 21, 39, 40, 58
Carlyle, Jane, 1, 12, 32
Carlyle, Thomas, 1, 12, 18-22, 23, 28, 31-34, 51, 62
Carne, Elizabeth (friend of C.F.), 31, 44, 53-54, 60
Coleridge, Hartley, 17, 23
Coleridge, Samuel Taylor, 11, 18, 19, 23, 24
Conolly, Dr., 35

Fox, Anna Maria (sister of C.F.), 8-10, 15, 21-22, 25, 29, 39, 45, 46, 48, 49-50, 52, 53, 55, 56, 57, 59, 60, 61, 62, 64, 65
Fox, Charles (uncle of C.F.), 11-12, 31-32
Fox, Elizabeth (née Tregelles, paternal grandmother of C.F.), 4, 5-6, 10
Fox, George Croker (nephew of C.F.), 56, 59
Fox, Gurney (nephew of C.F.), 52, 56, 60
Fox, Henry (nephew of C.F.), 55-56, 59
Fox, Jane (née Backhouse, sister-in-law of C.F.), 29, 51-53, 55-56, 58
Fox, Jane Backhouse (niece of C.F.), 56
Fox, Joanna (née Flannering), 12
Fox, Joshua (uncle of C.F.), 12
Fox, Maria (née Barclay, mother of C.F.), 6-7, 8, 10, 29, 42, 50, 53-54
Fox, Robert (nephew of C.F.), 56, 59
Fox, Robert Barclay (brother of C.F.), 2, 8-9, 14, 15, 16, 18, 20, 21, 25-27, 38, 50, 51-53, 57, 58
Fox, Robert Were (father of C.F.), 3-5, 9, 10, 14, 29, 54, 55, 56, 60
Fox, Samuel Middleton (cousin of C.F.), 1, 5, 11
Fox, Sarah (née Hustler, Aunt Charles), 11-12, 31-32, 58
Fox, Sarah (née Lloyd, Aunt Alfred), 11
Friends Italian Schools, 55, 65-66
Fry, Elizabeth (cousin of C.F.), 1, 6, 35, 46

GARIBALDI, Giuseppe, 55, 65
Gurney, Joseph (great uncle of C.F.), 6
Gurney, Joseph John (cousin of C.F.), 3
Gurney, Priscilla, 6
Gurney, Rachel, see Barclay, Rachel
HARE, Rev. Julius, 18-19, 22, 26, 28
Hodgkin, Lucy (née Fox, cousin of C.F.), 28, 58, 59, 66
Hodgkin, Thomas, 28, 59
Holdsworth, L. Violet, 25-26
Hunt, Holman, 57
INFANT SCHOOL, 46-47
JORDAN, Thomas (drawing master), 9
KINGSLEY, Charles, 40, 42-43
Kisting (Prussian sailor), 47
LAURENCE, Samuel, 37
MATAMOROS, Manuel, 60
Maurice, Frederick Denison, 19, 28, 39-40, 43-45, 46
Mill, John Stuart, 1, 29-31, 39, 40-41, 43, 48
Moultrie, John, 15
NIGHTINGALE, Florence, 46
PENJERRICK, 14, 59
Pym, Horatio (Horace) Noble, 1, 2, 8, 13, 41, 66
RICHARDS, John (tutor), 9
Rogers, Maria (friend of C.F.), 29, 51, 52
Rosehill, Falmouth, 3, 9, 14
Royal Cornwall Polytechnic Society, 11, 29, 46, 47-48, 59
Royal Cornwall Sailors' Home, 46, 47, 62-64
Rundall, Samuel (Rundell, Samuel), 42
SCHIMMEL-PENNINCK, Mary Anne, 8
Schleiermacher, Friedrich Daniel Ernst, 44-45
Shelley, Percy Bysshe, 23, 26, 36, 37
Stephen, Caroline Emelia, 41, 54, 58, 64
Sterling, Edward, 19, 25
Sterling, John, 13, Chapter V passim, 28, 29, 30, 31, 32, 36-37, 39, 40-41, 43, 44, 48, 58, 67
Sterling, Susannah (Susan), (wife of John Sterling) 18, 19, 22, 23, 24-25
TENNYSON, Alfred, Lord, 1, 57
Torrijos, General, 19
Tregelles, Elizabeth, see Fox, Elizabeth
Tuckett, Mariana, 64
VERRAN, Michael, 32-34
Victoria, Queen, 3, 17
WORDSWORTH, William, 1, 11-12, 16, 17, 22, 23, 34-35
YEARLY MEETINGS of the Society of Friends, 10-11, 17, 30, 32, 37, 42, 45, 53

76